The Passion of the Christ
and
His Mother

Including
The Linkage with Exodus and
the Night of the Passover

The Passion of the Christ and His Mother

Including
The Linkage with Exodus and
the Night of the Passover

Professor Courtenay Bartholomew, M.D.

Queenship
PUBLISHING COMPANY
P.O. Box 220 • Goleta, CA 93116
(800) 647-9882 • (805) 692-0043 • Fax: (805) 967-5133
www.queenship.org

Library of Congress Number # 2004101515

Published by:
    Queenship Publishing
    P.O. Box 220
    Goleta, CA 93116
    (800) 647-9882 • (805) 692-0043 • Fax: (805) 967-5133
    www.queenship.org

Printed in the United States of America

ISBN: 1-57918-249-6

Table of Contents

The Roman Catholic Archdiocese of Port of Spain

27 Maraval Road, Port of Spain, Trinidad and Tobago

ARCHBISHOP'S OFFICE
Telephone: 868-622-1103
Fax: 868-622-1165
E-mail: abishop@carib-link.net

031/04   February 6, 2004.

Professor Courtenay Bartholomew,
Medical Research Centre,
7 Queen's Park East,
Port of Spain.

Dear Professor Bartholomew,

I finished reading the final draft of your new book, *The Passion of Christ and His Mother Mary*. As always, interesting reading.

With this letter, I grant approval, i.e. the Imprimatur for the printing of the book, *The Passion of Christ and His Mother Mary.*

Congratulations on your latest accomplishment. I look forward to your next book.

With every best personal wish, I am,

Sincerely yours in the Lord,

Most Reverend Edward J. Gilbert C.Ss.R.
Archbishop of Port of Spain

EJG/ma

Dedication

To my mother Marie, who had a great devotion to Our Lady and who died while praying the Rosary in her final asthmatic respiratory distress.

An Appreciation

I wish to the express my appreciation and sincere thanks to Ms. Janie Garza for the privilege of inviting me to be in her company during her experience of the Passion of Our Lady on Good Friday, 2003 in Austin, Texas, which encouraged me to write this book.

**Janie Garza and her spiritual director
Fr. Henry Bordeaux after an apparition.**

Acknowledgement

My thanks and gratitude also to Ms. Camille Jackman and Ms. Mary Alcala-Jack for the typing of this manuscript, and to Sir Ellis Clarke and Ms. Mary Pinder for proofreading the text at such short notice.

Introduction

The Gospels speak very briefly about the Crucifixion. For example, all that Matthew had to write about the Crucifixion was: "Upon arriving at the site called Golgotha, they gave him a drink of wine flavoured with gall, which he tasted but refused to drink. When they had crucified him, they divided his clothes among them by casting lots" (Matthew 27:33-35). Mark was no more expansive: "It was the third hour and they crucified him" (Mark 15:25). Luke, although he was a physician, added nothing to the brief account of Matthew and Mark. John, the beloved disciple, was the only one who was at the foot of the Cross. He also says no more than the others, except to add that "one of the soldiers thrust the lance into his side, and immediately blood and water flowed out" (John 19:34).

Truly great people are always humble, and Jesus also chose for a mother the most humble of women: "My soul magnifies the Lord and my spirit rejoices in God my Savior; because he has regarded the humility of his handmaid…" (Luke 1:46-55). True humility does not boast and does not seek applause and so, as far as heaven was concerned, it was enough simply to say: "They crucified him." But in so stating in that era of history, the people certainly knew what it meant to be crucified.

Crucifixion was not abolished until 337 AD by Constantine the Great, but no one who was crucified was ever tortured and degraded like the Nazarene was; he who chose for himself his mode of death. Of course, he could have chosen to be stoned to death or decapitated with a sword, but those forms of death would not do. The greatest love in creation history had to experience the greatest suffering, and his suffering was, in turn, his greatest act of love.

Undoubtedly, it was Mary who taught the apostles about the birth of Jesus and many other things, and I am sure that she also instructed them not to write too much about herself because it was to be the Gospel of her son, not of Mary! But as John wrote in the conclusion of his Gospel: "There are still many things that Jesus did, if they were all written in detail, I don't think the world itself would contain the books which would have to be written" (John 21:25). And so, God, in his purposeful wisdom, while choosing to speak to us first and foremost through the Holy Scriptures, also speaks to us through the teachings of the Church and through private revelations.

Now, there is a time and a season for everything and I truly feel that Mr. Mel Gibson's film *The Passion of the Christ* is all-timely in this era of destructive brinkmanship and threatening annihilation of nations (some do not like us to use the word 'apocalyptic'!), religious conflict, fundamentalism and fanaticism — sometimes done in the name of God!

I am told that Mel Gibson researched the *Passion of Our Lord* as written by the Venerable Anne Catherine Emmerich in her four-volume writings on *The Life of Jesus Christ and Biblical Revelations*. She was born on September 8, 1774 at Flamske near Koesfeld, Westphalia in West Germany, and became a nun of the Augustinian Order on November 13, 1803. She died on February 9, 1824, and for most of her later years she subsisted for long periods almost entirely on water and the Holy Eucharist. Her privileged and mystical visions provide a wealth of information not found in the Bible, not surprisingly so when one considers the ending of St. John's Gospel!

She was told by God that her gift of seeing past, present and future was greater than that possessed by anyone else in history at that time. From that year until her death, she bore the stigmata of Our Lord, including a cross over her heart and wounds from the crown of thorns. During the last five years of her life, the day-by-day transcription of visions and mystical experiences was recorded by Clemens Brentano, a poet and literary leader at the time, who, from the time he met her, abandoned his distinguished career and devoted the rest of his life to that work.

The Life of Jesus Christ and Biblical Revelations is one of the most extraordinary books ever to be published. These four volumes record the visions of the famous mystic, who was privileged to behold innumerable events of biblical times, going back all the way to the creation of the world as she describes persons, places, events and traditions in intimate detail. It is a work that over a century has made conversions, encouraged vocations for religious life and inspired thousands of people to a fonder love of their faith. These revelations constitute one of the greatest treasures of Catholic mystical writings. It was a special gift of Divine Providence and an extraordinary favour granted by God for this confused and unbelieving age.

The Mystical City of God by the Venerable Mother Mary of Jesus of Agreda (Maria de Jesus de Agreda) (1602 – 1665) is another monumental four volume, 2,676 pages history of the life of the Blessed Virgin Mary, as revealed by Our Lady to this 17th Spanish Carmelite nun [FRANCISCAN]. Venerable Mary saw in ecstasy all the events and later Our Lady told her to write them down in a book, which was eventually acclaimed by popes, cardinals and theologians. More than just the life of the Blessed Virgin Mary, her visions and writings also contained information on the creation of the world, the meaning of the Apocalypse, Lucifer's rebellion and the hidden life of Jesus, Mary and Joseph. She is also known to have had the gift of bilocation and there has been much reliable evidence that over a period of eleven years from 1620 to 1631, she was frequently seen by the Indians of America in that era, teaching them the faith and because of the mantle which she wore, she was known to them as "The Lady in Blue". In 1988, I visited the Convent of the Immaculate Conception in Sorce, Spain where the incorrupt body of the deceased Carmelite [FRANCISCAN] now lies.

Another mystic, whom I have quoted in this book, is Maria Valtorta. She was born on March 14, 1897 in Caserta, Italy and died on October 12, 1961, in her 65th year of life. Following a severe injury to her back, she spent most of her life in illness and she did most of her writings when lying in bed. Indeed, she once selected the phrase to be printed in her memory. It was: "I have finished suffering, but I will go on loving." Pope Pius XII ordered her book the *Poem of the Man God* to be published in 1948, but, like the writings of all other well-known mystics, including Maria de Jesus of Agreda and St. Faustina Kowalska of Poland, the reading of their writings were initially discouraged. However, as Bishop Roman Danylak, Titular Bishop of Nyssa, Rome, wrote on June 24, 2001: "This major work of Maria Valtorta, the *Poem of the*

Man-God, is the Gospel expanded, and with her other writings, is in perfect consonance with the canonical Gospels, with the traditions and the magisterium of the Catholic Church."

Notably and significantly, at the beginning of her mystical visions and experiences, on 16 August, 1944 Jesus began by praising his mother with these words: "Today write only this. Purity has such a value that the womb of a creature can contain the Uncontainable One, because she possessed the greatest purity that a creature of God could have. The Most Holy Trinity descended with Its perfections, inhabited with Its Three Persons, enclosed Its infinity in a small space. But It did not debase Itself by so doing, because the love of the Virgin and the will of God widened the space until they rendered it a Heaven... Eve had been created spotless but she wanted to become corrupt of her own free will. Mary, who lived in a corrupt world (Eve was in a pure world), did not wish to violate her purity, not even with one thought remotely connected with sin. She knew that sin exists. She saw its various and horrible forms and implications. She saw them all, including the most hideous one: deicide. But she knew them solely to expiate them and to be forever the woman who has mercy on sinners and prays for their redemption. This thought will be the introduction to other holy things that I will give for your benefit and the welfare of many people."

I am sure that viewing the true Passion of Our Lord will impress and convert many, and many will also learn to be more grateful to him for his sacrifice for our sake. But it is my hope that the reader will also become more appreciative and knowledgeable about the "martyrdom" of his mother and the reason *why* they *both* had to suffer, albeit differently, for the redemption of mankind, as was foretold in the Scriptures.

I have not seen Mr. Gibson's film at the time of writing this book, but having read many years ago the visions of the detailed Passion of Our Lord and of Our Lady through the writings of various privileged mystics, I am certain that what is to be shown in the film, as tear-jerking as it may be, is nonetheless significantly less horrid than what Christ actually had to endure. Indeed, it would have been imprudent, indiscreet and perhaps irresponsible to portray it on film in all its brutality. Among other things, it would then have to be rated: "For adults only."

I have been very privileged to have been invited by Ms. Janie Garza to be with her at her bedside on Good Friday, 2003. Janie Garza of Austin, Texas, wife and mother, was chosen by the Lord to be a vessel of simple and holy messages for the family of today. These messages are given by the Holy Family — Jesus, Mary and Joseph. Janie has been receiving messages since February 15, 1989. As Fr. Henry Bordeaux OCD, wrote in October 1994: "I can testify that since I became her spiritual director nearly five years ago, I have seen immense growth in virtue in her, in her husband and in her sons, two of whom are teenagers. The purpose of these messages is no doubt to help Christian families to become holy families. Thus, Our Lady teaches us from her own experience as wife and mother, being, of course, full of grace." For several years now, Janie, as a victim soul, has experienced the Passion of Our Lord. In 2003, however, she experienced part of the Passion of his mother. I was there to witness it. The Passion of the Christ and his Mother was too horrible for words! Were you there when they crucified my Lord?

The Venerable Anne Catherine Emmerich

**The Venerable Maria
de Jesus de Agreda**

Maria Valtorta

Chapter 1

On Suffering

"If any man would come after me, let him deny himself and take up his cross and follow me" (Matthew 16:24).

God, who is Love, gave us a free will to love and respect his commands. According to Christian belief, the first entrance of evil into the created order came through the sin of the angels, which introduced disharmony and conflict into God's creation. Sin, it is believed, not only has personal but cosmic consequences. And so, the whole created world, not only sinful mankind, stands in need of redemption from sin and the effects of sin. Satan and his followers sinned freely. So did Adam and Eve. So do we all. Indeed, our free will distances God from any responsibility for sin and its consequences.

No one can be coerced into loving another. It must be freely given. As Russel Shaw wrote in his book *Does Suffering Make Sense?,* love either comes freely or it does not exist at all. God could have created a world of obedient and subservient robots but that would have excluded love as well as free will. Such an imposition on man would have been too high a price to pay to make love possible. Indeed, the Crucifixion and the death of Jesus Christ was the greatest act of love in world history. It was all about love: "God so loved the world that he gave his only begotten son, so that whoever believes in him may not die but may have eternal life" (John 3:16). In fact, anyone who fails to love can never have known God, because God is love (1 John 4:8). But, as it happens, true love needs to suffer and love is strengthened by the tears of suffering. As Peter Kreeft observed in his treatise *Making Sense Out Of Suffering*, see how close joy is to tears for when joy is overflowing, we also burst into tears!

Love certainly calls for sacrifices since love and sacrifice go hand in hand and there can often be no great love without sacrifice, without suffering. St. Therese of Lisieux knew this and in a letter to her sister, she once wrote: "Let us not imagine a love without suffering and bitter suffering too." Many also do not understand what they consider to be the folly of the Cross. In fact, as Kreeft also wrote, "even Satan did not expect this folly." But, this foolish heart loves us so much even when his love is not returned and he suffers in silence the magnitude of our ingratitude.

True love is always willing to suffer. As St. Phillip Neri once said: "The Cross is a gift which God gives to his friend." The acceptance of suffering is grace. The Cross is grace. It is all about humility and once when asked what were the four cardinal virtues, St. Bernard of Clairvaux replied: "Humility, humility, humility and humility." Take my yoke upon your shoulders and learn from me; for. I am meek and humble in heart (Matthew 11:29).

In fact, the mystery of suffering stands out with unique starkness in the life of Jesus Christ. To the non-Christian, the suffering of Jesus seems at first glance to make little or no sense and it sometimes constitutes an insuperable obstacle to faith. This observation is recorded by Paul in 1 Cor. 1:22-25: "And so, while the Jews demand miracles and Greeks look for wisdom, here are we preaching Christ crucified; to the Jews an obstacle that they cannot get over, to the pagans madness, but to those who have been called, whether they are Jews or Greeks, a Christ who is the power and wisdom of God. For God's foolishness is wiser than human wisdom, and God's weakness is stronger than human strength."

And so, there are certain religions, which, among many other things, would not accept that Jesus Christ is the Son of God, if only because of his ignoble crucifixion and death. How could the Almighty God subject himself to such degradation? How can this great God lower himself to become man? How can he who is omnipotent choose to be so impotent? How could the Creator of life die? And how can God be born of a lowly woman? But greatness, true greatness and humility walk hand in hand and so he was "meek and humble of heart."

Indeed, the Christian value of suffering is found in Jesus' own words: "He who will not take up his cross and follow me is not worthy of me (Matthew 10:38), and he also added: "If any man would come after me, let him deny himself and take up his cross and follow me. For whoever would save his life will lose it; and whoever loses his life for my sake and the gospel's will save it" (Matthew 16:24-25).

Suffering is the iron which passes through the fire to become steel. It strengthens character, fosters conversion and leads us to recognize and accept our dependence upon God. But there is good reason to bear suffering. It is the price we often have to pay for the glory of the afterlife. The crown is never attained except through struggle and sacrifice. Suffering is a purgative experience. "I consider that the sufferings of this present time are not worth comparing with the glory that is to be revealed to us," said Paul to the Romans (Romans 8:18). And so, towards the end of his suffering life, while he was a prisoner in Rome, he wrote to Timothy: "I have finished the race, I have kept the faith. From now on a merited crown awaits me" (2 Timothy 4:7-8).

So said, it is the hope of "resurrection" that makes it possible for us to sustain the agony of suffering and death and the resurrection of Jesus Christ is the incontrovertible reward of redemption. In a letter to the Hebrews, Paul also said: "As it was his purpose to bring a great many of his sons to glory, it was appropriate of God, for whom everything exists and through whom everything exists, should make perfect, through suffering, the leader who would take them to their salvation by his passion" (Hebrews 2:10). He was talking about the Redeemer. But co-suffering with him beneath his Cross was the mother.

But this topic of suffering is certainly not a scientific one although science has enlightened us somewhat on the mechanism of pain. Pain and suffering in some cases is mediated through neural elements and there are endorphins even in earthworms. This indicates that they suffer pain but it is believed that pain becomes less intense as we go down the phylogenetic spectrum and that it is often not as acute in the non-human as in the human family. In fact, there was suffering in the biological world for long epochs even before humans came on the scene. And so, it can be said that what happens to humans has happened to every living thing. The whole of creation involved suffering. It is rooted in the very nature of things. But human nature must be cultivated and has to learn to appreciate that there are mountains to climb before achieving perfection. Therefore, it must be shaped and chastened by the hammer of adversities and refined in the crucible of suffering and tribulations in order that it may also learn to despise worldly goods as the be-all and end-all of human existence.

Animals, however, do not have pain in childbirth as we do. According to Genesis, this pain was one of the results of the fall and the meaning and purpose of suffering in history is that it leads to repentance which man needed to make after the fall. In fact, history has frequently witnessed that only after suffering do nations and individuals turn back to God, albeit sometimes only for a while until the next suffering! Indeed, suffering does bring repentance. As C. S. Lewis once said: "Pain is God's megaphone to rouse a dulled world."

Indeed, as narrated in both Testaments of the Bible, to be chosen by God is not to be protected from suffering. It is to travel the road from Gethsemane to Calvary. It is often to suffer and to be chastised, strengthened and delivered as one passes through it. In fact, as Leon Bloy once wrote: "When you ask God to send you trials, you may be sure your prayer will be granted." This, unfortunately, is what unbelievers like Nietzsche (1844-1900) neither fathomed nor sought the grace to understand, and so, he once said: "What really raises one's indignation against suffering is not suffering intrinsically but the senselessness of suffering." There can indeed be senseless suffering but not all suffering is senseless.

Every life is chastened, christened and straightened in struggle. Indeed, everywhere there is vicarious suffering and all world progress and history is ultimately brought under the shadow of a cross. The story, therefore, was a passion play long before Christ arrived on the world scene, and since the beginning of time myriads creatures have been giving up their lives as a ransom for many. The ram which was sacrificed in place of Isaac and the many lambs immolated in the Temple are some of the many examples in relatively recent times. In that sense, Jesus is not the exception to the natural order but the chief and high exemplification of it. It was the martyrdom of the God-man. Creation has known of no greater sacrifice, no greater suffering, physical, emotional or spiritual, and no greater love.

A fellow medical scientist, Dr. Tagashi Nagi, the pioneer professor of radiology at the University of Nagasaki in Japan, suffered and died of atomic disease 6 years after the second atomic bomb fell on his homeland on August 9, 1945. He once reflectively said: "Unless you have suffered and wept you really do not understand what compassion is nor can you give comfort to someone who is suffering. If you have not cried you cannot dry another's eyes. Unless you have walked in darkness you cannot help wanderers find their way. Unless you have looked into the eyes of menacing death, you cannot help another rise from the dead and taste anew of the joy of being alive."

Samuel Butler once wrote: "Poets by their suffering grow...." But suffering is often a means for growth in holiness. While it is not something to be sought after, for even Christ in his humanity, while he bore extreme suffering in Gethsemane, he also prayed: Father, take this cup away from me, but not my will but what you will" (Mark. 14:36). In fact, it is this complete resignation and acceptance which makes suffering especially redemptive. As Pope John Paul II said: "Christ has taught man to do good by his suffering and to do good to those who suffer. In this double aspect he has completely revealed the meaning of suffering."

Matthew also wrote about the suffering of Jesus to come: "From that time Jesus began to show his disciples that he must go to Jerusalem and suffer many things from the elders and chief priests and scribes and be killed, and on the third day be raised" (Mt. 16:21). This message, needless to say, was not well-received by those closest to him. They were looking for an all-conquering Messiah-King, who would restore Israel to greatness. But, as Pope John Paul II wrote: "Precisely by means of his Cross, he must accomplish the work of salvation."

And so, as part of his redemptive act, he took upon himself physical pain and suffering and the personal desolation of the state of sin. As Paul wrote: "For our sake he made himself to be sin who knew no sin, so that in him, we might become the righteousness of God" (2 Cor. 5:21). But Isaiah had prophesied the sacrifice of Jesus centuries before: "And yet ours were the sufferings he bore, ours the sorrow carried. But we, thought of him as someone punished, struck by God, and brought low. Yet he was bruised through our faults, crushed for our sins; upon him lies the punishment that brings us peace, and through his wounds we are healed" (Isaiah 53: 4-5).

Indeed, there is nothing in life more difficult to understand and accept than the suffering of the innocent, but as Martin Luther King once said: "Suffering is redemption, especially unearned suffering." In Jesus Christ it is precisely this experience of innocent suffering that is the instrument for redemption. The rationale is that we have incurred a debt to God, namely, the punishment due to sin. Christ offered to pay our debt for us and the Father accepted. Jesus grieved, suffered, died on the Cross and the debt is paid. He was the ultimate scapegoat. We are redeemed.

Paraphrasing St. Thomas Aquinas in his *Summa Theologica,* Fr. Gerald Farfan, in his textbook *A Biblical Course of Religious Instruction*, explains why God became man to redeem us all: "When man rebelled against God, God's justice required adequate reparation be made; justice meaning 'giving to everyone his due.' But since God is infinite, an infinite insult was made to him when man rebelled against him, and if the reparation was to be adequate, that is, if justice were to be satisfied, such an insult required infinite reparation. Justice also required that the reparation be offered by man, but man is a finite being and incapable of making infinite reparation. Left to himself, therefore, man would forever be separated from God. The only solution to the impasse was that the infinite God should become man, and as man offer reparation to God. Since the person offering the reparation was himself infinite, the reparation would equal the crime and man could once more be united in friendship with God. So, in his loving mercy, God sent his son to make reparation for the sin of man: 'God so loved the world that he sent his only begotten son…' " (John 3:16).

The Bible also briefly states: "There stood by the cross of Jesus, his mother and the disciple standing by…" (John 19:25) This grossly underestimates the unspeakable anguish of the mother beneath the Cross as she stood by helplessly and watched her beloved son suffer and die the most excruciating of all deaths. In fact, she participated as fully as possible in her son's Passion and death. As Pope John Paul pointed out, Mary was called "to share in a singular and unrepeatable way in the very mission of her son. Her ascent of Calvary and her standing at the foot of the Cross together with the beloved disciple were a special sort of sharing in the redeeming death of her son."

Chapter 2

The Fall of the Angels

The sacrifice and Passion of the Christ cannot be fully understood without a knowledge of the creation story and the entrance of sin into God's creation. The seven "day" story of creation is recorded in the Book of Genesis but only brief mention is made of the fall of the angels in the Bible. For example, Isaiah spoke briefly of the fall of Satan: "How did you come to fall from the heavens, Daystar, son of Dawn? How did you come to be thrown to the ground, you who enslaved the nations? You who used to think to yourself, 'I will climb up to the heavens; and higher than the stars of God I will set my throne. I will sit on the Mount of Assembly in the recesses of the north. I will climb to the top of thunderclouds, I will rival the Most High. What! Now you have fallen to Sheol, to the very bottom of the abyss!" (Isaiah 14:12-15). In the New Testament, Luke records the words of Jesus himself: "I watched Satan fall like lightning from heaven" (Luke 10:18).

In *The Mystical City of God* written by the Venerable Maria de Jesus of Agreda (1602-1665), the mystic relates in great detail the account of the creation of the angels and the role of Mary, the Mother of the Word, as predestined by God. She wrote in Book 1, Chapter 1 that in the beginning God created heaven and earth. He created heaven for angels and men, and the earth as a place of pilgrimage for mortals. The angels were created in the Empyrean heavens and in a state of grace by which they might be first to merit the reward of glory. At first, they received a more explicit intelligence of the Being of God, one in substance, three in person, and they were commanded to adore and reverence him as their Creator.

Heaven and earth were hardly created when God dared to reveal his divine plan for the first time, also proposing it as a test for the angelic creatures. The angels were then informed that he was to create a human nature and reasoning creatures lower than themselves and that they too should love and reverence him as their author. They were informed that these lower creatures were to stand in high favour and that the Second Person of the Blessed Trinity was to become incarnate and assume their nature, raising it to the hypostatic union, and that the angels were also to acknowledge him as their head, not only as God, but as God and man, the God-Man, adoring him and reverencing him.

To this command, using their free will, all the obedient and holy angels submitted themselves and they gave their full assent and acknowledgment with a humble and loving subjection of the will. But Lucifer, the brightest and the most beautiful of the angels, full of envy and pride, resisted and induced his followers to resist likewise, as they in reality did, preferring to follow him and disobey the divine command. But after it was revealed to the angels that they would have to obey the Incarnate Word, a third precept was given to them, namely, that they were to admit as a superior conjointly with him, a woman in whose womb the Only Begotten of the Father was to assume flesh, and that this woman was to be their Queen and the Queen of all creatures. He then presented her to them, not in reality, since she did not as yet exist, but in a sign or image. It was a woman, adorned with the sun, standing on the moon, and with twelve stars on her head for a crown. St. John describes this image in the Book of Revelation (Rev. 12:1-2). This woman was shown in her condition of motherhood, that is, in a state of maternity. The angelic spirits understood at once the role of this woman.

The mystic went on to relate that the good angels obeyed this latter command of the Lord with still increasing humility, praising the powers and the mysteries of the Most High, accepting also the woman of the sign as their Queen. Lucifer and his confederates, on the other hand, rose to a higher pitch of pride and boastful insolence. In disorderly fury, he aspired to be himself the head of all the human race and of the angelic orders, and if there were to be a hypostatic union, he demanded that it be consummated in him: "It is only I who will be like the Most High. All will render me honour," he shouted. Above all, the decree constituting him inferior to the mother of the Incarnate Word, he opposed with horrible blasphemies. Turning against God in unbridled indignation and calling upon the other angels, he exhorted them, saying: "Unjust are these commands and injury is done to my greatness. This human nature which you, Lord, look upon with so much love and which you favour so highly, I will persecute and destroy. To this end I will direct all my power and all my aspirations. And this woman, Mother of the Word, I will hurl from the pedestal upon which you have proposed to place her and at my hands, the plan which you set up shall come to naught."

This proud boast aroused the indignation of the Lord and to humiliate and punish him, he spoke thus to Lucifer: "This woman whom you refuse to honour shall crush your head and by her shall you be vanquished and annihilated. And if through your pride, death enters into the world, life and salvation of mortals shall enter through the humility of this woman. Those that are of the nature and likeness of this man and woman shall enjoy the gifts and the crowns which you and your followers have lost." Then happened that great battle in heaven which St. John describes in Revelation 12. The good angels, led in battle by Michael the Archangel, cast one third of the angelic host down to earth. It was the first warfare in creation history, a war beyond human imagination; a disaster unparalleled in eternity and in time. It stemmed from the free will which God in his wisdom had chosen to give his creatures, both angelic and mortal.

Chapter 3

From Adam and Eve to Moses and the Passover

In the fullness of time, as recorded in the Book of Genesis, God said: "Let us make man in our own image, in the likeness of ourselves... God saw all that he had made, and indeed it was very good. Evening came and morning came; the sixth day" (Genesis 1:26; 1:31). Eventually, when the earth was "user-friendly" for man, God formed Adam from the dust of the ground and placed him in the Garden of Eden. He then said to him: "Of all the trees in the garden you may freely eat but of the tree of the knowledge of good and evil you shall not eat, for in the day that you eat thereof you will surely die." God then caused a deep sleep to fall upon Adam and took one of his ribs and closed up the flesh. One may well say that it was the first biblical record of anaesthesiology and surgery. A companion was given to Adam, who then said: "This one is bone of my bones and flesh of my flesh. She shall be called woman because she was taken out of man" (Genesis 2:21-23). He called her Eve, meaning "mother of all the living" (Genesis 3:20).

In due course, Satan then tempted Eve first and said to her: "You surely will not die. For God knows that in the day you eat thereof your eyes will be opened and you will be as gods knowing good and evil." It was reflective of Satan's perpetual obsession to be 'like God'! Eve then ate of the fruit and gave it to Adam and he did eat. Satan had his first victory over mortals. Sin had entered the world for the first time. God then rebuked the ancient serpent and said to him: "Because you have done this, cursed are you above all cattle and above all wild animals; upon your belly you shall go and dust you shall eat all the days of your life. I will put enmity between you and the woman, between your seed and her seed. She will crush your head and you will strike at her heel" (Genesis 3:14 -15).

It was God's first promise to man that he will redress the situation. The "woman" about whom he spoke could certainly not have been the first Eve whom Satan had just seduced. Satan knew that full well. He had heard that rebuke when he saw her in image form clothed with the sun before he fell from heaven. It was the woman of Revelation 11:19; 12:1 whom he saw in an image before his fall: "Then the temple of God in heaven was opened, and the ark of the covenant was seen inside his temple... And a great sign appeared in heaven, a woman clothed with the sun, with the moon under her feet and on her head a crown of twelve stars...." This therefore was the woman predestined to crush the head of Satan. But she was not to be born on earth until eons later, around 16 BC.

In time Adam and Eve gave birth to Cain and Abel and out of jealousy Cain killed Abel. It was history's first recorded murder. With the passing of time, Cain and his wife gave birth to Enoch. Enoch's son, Irad, became the father of Mehujael, who in turn became the father of Methushaen, and so on. But as the centuries went by, it seemed that the more people there were on earth, the more wickedness there was and scarcely any man or woman gave thought to the Lord who had created them. In fact, they became so thoughtless that they no longer knew what was right nor did they seem to care. The earth was corrupt in God's sight and was filled with violence. Indeed, when the Lord saw that the wickedness of mankind was so great on earth, he was sorry that he had made man. But Noah found favour in the sight of the Lord.

The well-known account of Noah and the Ark is recorded in the Book of Genesis. Now, when God destroyed the earth by the great flood of forty days, he said to Noah: "I will establish my covenant with you, and with your descendants after you... There shall be no flood to destroy the earth again. This is the sign of the covenant that I make between me and you and every living creature with you for all generations; I set my bow in the clouds, and it shall be a sign of the covenant between me and the earth. When I gather the clouds over the earth and the bow appears in the clouds, I will remember my covenant between me and you and every living creature of every kind. And so, the waters shall never again become a flood to destroy all things of flesh."

Noah himself lived for 350 years after the flood. At the age of

950 years, he died knowing that his sons were to be the fathers of the nations of the world. Shem's five sons were to be to fathers of the Semitic people or Hebrews and from his line would spring two upright men called Abram and Lot. Ham's four sons would go forth and people Africa and would also be the fathers of the non-Hebrew inhabitants of Canaan. From Japateh's seven sons came the Gentiles or the non-Jewish nations. Thus were the families of the sons of Noah separated into the nations of the world.

The story of Abram and Sarai is recorded in Genesis 12-23. Such was its importance that its history covers more space in the Genesis account than does that of the entire human race from creation down to their time. At the request of the Lord, Abram eventually settled in the land of Canaan when he left Ur, where there were pagans and idol worshippers who believed themselves to be specially favoured by the moon god. Abram was obedient to the Lord and was willing to forsake home and country for the unknown with his wife Sarai ever at his side. This was about 1850 BC.

Now, God had told him that he was to be the father of many nations and thus his name would change and instead of being Abram, which means "exalted father," he became Abraham, which meant "father of a multitude." Sarai, too, had to change her name. Her new name would be Sarah, meaning "Princess."

Eventually, because of her long barrenness, with Sarah's approval, Abraham begat a child through his Egyptian maidservant Hagar. He was named Ishmael. However, when Abraham was 100 years old a son was born to him and Sarah. This was Isaac. Eventually God tested the faith of Abraham, the founder of the Hebrew race, from which the Saviour of the world was expected to come. "Abraham," he said to him, "take your son Isaac, your only son, and bring him with you to the land of Moriah. There you will give him up to me as a burnt offering upon a mountain that I will show to you."

Grieved and heart-broken as he was, Abraham had faith in the Lord and did not question him. He took the wood for the burnt offering and laid it on Isaac's shoulder to carry, and father and son went off together to climb the mountain where the offering would be made. When they came to the place on the top of the mountain that God had told him about, Abraham built an altar of stone and laid the wood upon it. He reached then for his son and tied his hands and feet. Then Abraham laid his son upon the wood of the altar and reached out his hand for the knife. He raised it slowly but when he brought the knife up high, ready for the downward plunge, the angel of the Lord called out to him: "Abraham, Abraham, do not lay your hand upon the boy. Do not harm him. Now I know that you fear God seeing that you have not withheld your son, your only son from him." Abraham lifted up his eyes, and behold, behind him was a ram, caught in a thicket by his horn. He gave a name to the place where he was prepared to sacrifice Isaac. He called it Jehovah-jireh, meaning "The Lord will provide."

As the years rolled by, Isaac bore children and grandchildren and great grandchildren and over the centuries the Hebrews grew greatly in numbers and lived in Egypt until a Pharaoh came into power and ordered all the Hebrews to be enslaved. It was in this captivity of over 400 years that the towering figure of the Old Testament arose, Moses. He was called by God to renew the covenant of Abraham and to lead his chosen people back to the Promised Land of Canaan. Moses then threatened Pharaoh: "Let my people go." When Pharaoh refused, Egypt was visited by ten plagues.

However, it was the tenth plague which eventually won the day for Israel. It was the death of the first-borns. God then decreed to the Israelites that a young lamb without blemish, a one year old male, was to be slaughtered and some of its blood daubed on the door posts of the houses. The Israelites were to eat the lamb hurriedly that same night with unleavened bread and bitter herbs for the Lord was to pass through the land of Egypt that night and strike down every first-born: "When I see the blood I will pass over you and no plague shall destroy you when I strike the land of Egypt" (Exodus 12:1-13).

Now, in Old Testament times almost all things according to the law were cleansed with blood and without the shedding of blood there was no remission. And so, by the sacrifice and blood of the Paschal lamb the Hebrews were delivered from Egyptian slavery and God himself laid down the ceremony of that sacrifice in keeping with his divine plan (Exodus 12:1-14). The lamb had to be male, for Christ, the true Paschal Lamb of God, was to be of that sex. It was one year old to foretell that Christ would be sacrificed in the early flower of his manhood. It had to be without spot, stain or blemish to foretell the sinlessness of Christ. The Hebrews fled from Egypt at night and were delivered from slavery to foretell how the Lord would be arrested at night, to be sacrificed and to deliver the world from the slavery of Satan.

The lamb's blood sprinkled on the doorposts pointed to Jesus' blood to be sprinkled on the Cross and, by which we were to be redeemed from sin, except that the killing of the unblemished lamb on that historic night in Egypt was merciful when compared to the dreadful Passion and crucifixion of the true Lamb of God, who voluntarily chose for himself the most painful and agonizing of deaths: "The Father loves me, because I lay down my life in order to take it up again. No one takes it from me; I lay it down of my own free will" (John 10:17-18).

Fr. James L. Meagher, D.D., in his book *How Christ Said The First Mass,* described how the Mass was foretold in the Passover ceremony of the Israelites. The word "Passover" comes from the Hebrew "Pesach", because in Egypt the Lord "passed over" the Israelites' houses signed with the blood of the Paschal lambs, when he killed the firstborn of every family and animal on the night of the Exodus. Now, this was the way the lamb was prepared since centuries before Christ. They washed the animal, foretelling the Passover washing performed by Christ and his Apostles, and with a rope they fastened the right forefoot of the lamb to the left hindfoot and the left forefoot to the right hindfoot, the cord making a cross emblematic of Christ fastened to his Cross. It was then skinned just as Christ was scourged almost skinless, and then, without breaking any of the bones, they drove a pomegranate stick through the tendons of its forefeet. They called this operation "the crucifying of the lamb," foretelling Christ crucified with his hands and feet nailed to the Cross. The victim they now named "the body of the lamb," to which Christ alluded at the Last Supper when He said: "This is my body" (Luke22:19).

Yahweh had also decreed to Moses and Aaron: "This is what is ordered for the Passover... It (the lamb) is to be eaten in one house alone, out of which house not a single morsel of flesh is to be eaten; nor must you break any bone of it" (Exodus 12:46-47). This was to foretell that while they would break the legs of the two thieves, not one bone of the true Lamb was to be broken (John 19:33). And so, Christ became the Pascal Lamb through whom we have been saved. He was killed, his blood was shed, his legs were not broken, his flesh was to be eaten (in the Eucharist).

The crucified lamb was placed in an oven lying on its cross. When cooked, the lamb was then placed on the table still lying on the cross. It was a striking prophetic portrait of the body of the dead Christ on the Cross, his skin all torn off by the flagellation, his blood and serum oozing out and then dried, making him look as though he had been roasted. This was the real portrait of Jesus on the Cross, not the aesthetic and comfortable-looking figure which is seen on crosses in churches and elsewhere.

Chapter 4

The Woman of Genesis 3:15 and Her Seed

Centuries later, in the fullness of time the "woman" of Genesis 3:15, the greatest of all women in the Bible, was born to Joachim and Anne of the tribe of David and a descendant of Abraham. According to the Venerable Catherine Emmerich, the first child born to Anne was a daughter but she was not the "child of the promise (covenant)." For seventeen years after the birth of their first child Anne was fruitless and prayed constantly and fervently for an end to her barrenness. Interestingly, it is often through initial barrenness that God has produced his great leaders in the Old Testament era. It is said that the Almighty could not find more worthy parents for his chosen bride and at last Anne gave birth to the "Immaculate Conception." Joachim and Anne, according to Catherine Emmerich, "lived together in continence afterwards and in the greatest devoutness and fear of the Lord."

In time God sent his messenger and ambassador Gabriel to a virgin in Nazareth with a gilt-edged invitation to her to be the "Mother of the Word." As the Gospel of Luke wrote: "In the sixth month, the angel Gabriel was sent from God to a town of Galilee called Nazareth, to a virgin betrothed to a man named Joseph, of the house of David, and the virgin's name was Mary. And coming to her he said: 'Hail, full of grace! The Lord is with you.' But she was greatly troubled by what was said and pondered what sort of greeting this might be. And the angel said to her, 'Do not be afraid, Mary, for you have found favour with God. Behold, you will conceive in your womb, and bear a son, and you shall name him Jesus. He will be great and will be called Son of the Most High, and the Lord God will give him the throne of David his father and he will rule over the house of Jacob forever, and of his kingdom there will be no end.' Mary then said to the angel, 'But how can this come about, since I am a virgin?' 'The Holy Spirit will come upon you'", the angel answered, 'and the power of the Most High will cover you with its shadow. And so the child would be holy and would be called Son of God. Know this too: your kinswoman Elizabeth has, in her old age, herself conceived a son, and she whom people call barren is now in her sixth month, for nothing is impossible to God.' 'I am the handmaid of the Lord,' said Mary, 'Let what you have said be done to me.' And the angel left her" (Luke 1:26-38).

Now, when she recovered her composure, she said "yes" to the invitation of Gabriel to be the Mother of the Word, the second Eve. The Holy Spirit then overshadowed her and she immediately conceived at that moment the God - Man, the second Adam. God's promise of Genesis 3:15 was being fulfilled. Redemption had begun. It was the marriage between heaven and earth. This daughter of the Father then also became the bride of the Holy Spirit and the mother of the Son. And so, with her, in her, and through her the Holy Spirit produced his most illustrious work, the Incarnation of the Word. The hypostatic union of the Son of God with human nature was accomplished and fulfilled as promised by God the Father before the fall of the angels from heaven. It was the most important event in human history. God so loved the world that he sent his only begotten son (John 3:16). Indeed, God also so loved the world and mankind that he made one of us his mother!

The first Eve was born out of the rib of the first Adam. The second Adam was born out of the womb of the second Eve. The first Eve said "yes" to Satan and sin. The second Eve said "yes" to Gabriel and God. Indeed, with her consent she played her part in what may be called 'God's conspiracy' to save the world from the dominion of Satan. It was the beginning of the "good news," but it was bad news for Satan. The Woman of Genesis 3:15 had consented! And with her consent two wondrous things happened. A woman, while remaining a virgin, became a mother, and more wondrous yet, a woman became the mother of her own Creator. On earth the Word had a mother without a father as in heaven he had a father without a mother. At that moment 'Infinity' confined himself in the womb of a mere mortal woman. The bodiless took upon himself a body; the invisible made himself visible; he who is without beginning began; the Son of God became the Son of Man. And prophecy was fulfilled: "Sacrifices and offerings you have not desired, but a body you have prepared for me... Lo, I have come to do your will, O God" (Hebrews 10:5-7).

It was said by the great homilist Fr. Leo Clifford on the Eternal Word Television Network (EWTN) that many years ago while preaching on the Blessed Virgin, Canon Sheehan of Ireland once gave this sermon: "It was decreed by God at the fall of our first parents that as their children would have inherited grace and glory if his commands had been obeyed, so, because of their disobedience, their children were to inherit only sin and shame. This law is universal. Not even the greatest saints were exempt from it. Once and once only did God create a soul as pure and beautiful at the moment of its conception as it is now in heaven; a soul to whom the Almighty could turn when weary of the deformity which sin had stamped upon mankind. It was the time when the fullness of years had come and it was decreed that the Son should leave the bosom of the Father and take flesh among men. For centuries, God had not created a soul in grace. Yes, he had fashioned and formed them and sent them into the world, but they were in the power of the enemy before they left his almighty hands. But now, for an instant, the old time was to come back again when God could look upon his work and say that it was good, and that it did not repent him that he had made it. And so, the Blessed Trinity fashioned and formed and sent into the world the soul of Mary. And God admired his handiwork, while hell trembled at the conception of the woman who was destined to break the power of its prince.

"This is the girl chosen from all women to give God the colour of his eyes and of his hair. She was to teach the Word to speak in her own accent. She was to help the Almighty walk his first baby steps. She was to give him the body and blood in which he would live and suffer and die to redeem us all. She was called Mary, a famous name in Jewish history, Miriam. Miriam was the sister of Moses and in God's inscrutable, providential plan Miriam helped Moses, the leader of the "exodus" from Egyptian slavery, grow. In the New Testament, the new Miriam, Mary, is going to help the Redeemer of the world to grow, to help to save us all. This time it was an "exodus", not from Egyptian slavery, but from the slavery of sin and Satan."

She was the sole human parent. No human father was involved and she alone furnished the sacred body of her son. She gave him his hands and feet which were to be pierced (Psalm 22:16) and the rib cage to be lanced, and just as the Son came eternally from the substance of the Father alone, so, too, in time, he came from the flesh and blood of Mary alone. As Fr. Michael O'Carrol of Dublin so scientifically put it: "His very genetic substance and constitution was Mary's. His DNA was totally Mary's." This body would be the instrument of redemption, for redemption was to come from suffering. Nine months later, she gave birth to the God-Man, the second Adam, "bone of her bones and flesh of her flesh," as the first Adam said about the first Eve. There was no room in the inn and so he was born in a humble stable, for where else would a lamb be born, even the Lamb of God, he, who was the most humble of all the lambs? He was born in Bethlehem, and so should it also be, for where else should the "Bread of Life" be born but in Bethlehem? Bethlehem means "House of Bread." And from her breasts she gave milk to this Bread of Life.

Thirty years later, the mother and her son were invited to a wedding banquet but the bride and groom were embarrassed. There was no more wine. "They have no wine," she told her son. "Woman, what concern is that to you and to me? My hour is not yet come," he replied to her. She, as it were, disregarded him and turning to the servants, she said: "Do whatever he tells you." It was then that he turned water, not only into wine, but into the best wine æ six jars full, about 120 gallons of it (John 2:12). However, she knew full well that by initiating his public ministry she would be hastening what she always feared most as his Calvary. Nonetheless, undoubtedly inspired by the Holy Spirit, she knew that the time had come. It was as though heavenly protocol demanded that it was the mother who should initiate his public ministry and hence the road which would also lead her to the foot of the Cross.

Chapter 5

The Last Supper

Three years later, as his ministry was approaching its end, there was another banquet which we call the Last Supper. From here onward I will quote verbatim part of the writings of the Venerable Anne Catherine Emmerich.

The Cenacle room for the Last Supper having being prepared, Peter and John went out of the Valley of Josephat and summoned Jesus and the apostles. The disciples and friends who were allowed to eat their Pasch in the Cenacle came later. Jesus and his followers were in three separate groups of twelve, each presided over by one who acted as the host, while Jesus and the twelve apostles were in the hall itself. Nathaniel and many of the older disciples were in one of the side rooms and in another with twelve more sat Eliacim, son of Cleophas and Mary Heli. He had been a disciple of John the Baptist. The mother of Jesus and the holy women were in one of the side buildings near the court of the Cenacle.

Three lambs had been immolated and sprinkled for them in the Temple but the fourth was slaughtered and sprinkled in the Cenacle. It was this lamb that Jesus ate with the twelve. Judas was not aware of these happenings as he had been engaged in various business affairs, among which was the plot to betray Jesus and consequently arrived only a few moments before the meal and after the immolation of the lamb had taken place.

The slaughter of the lamb for Jesus and the apostles was a most touching scene. It took place in the anteroom of the Cenacle. The apostles were chanting Psalm 118 (the psalm usually sung as the procession entered the Temple). Jesus spoke of a new period about to begin and said that the sacrifice of Moses and the significance of the Paschal lamb were about to be fulfilled, that on this account the lamb must be immolated as formerly in Egypt and that now they were ready to go forth from the house of bondage.

All the necessary vessels and instruments were now prepared. Then a beautiful little lamb was brought in and around its neck there was a garland which was taken off and sent to the Blessed Virgin, who was a little distance away with the other women. The lamb was then bound, its back on a little board and with a cord passed around the body. It reminded me of Jesus bound to the pillar. Simeon's son held the lamb's head up and Jesus then stuck it in the head with a knife, which he handed to Simeon's son that he might complete the slaughter. Jesus appeared quite timid in wounding the lamb as if it caused him much anguish. His movement was quick, his manner grave. The blood was then caught in a basin and the attendants brought a branch of hyssop, which Jesus dipped into it. Then, stepping to the door of the hall, he signed the two posts and the lock with the blood and stuck the bloody branch on the lintel of the door. He then uttered a few solemn words, saying, among other things: "The destroying angel shall pass by here. Without fear and anxiety, you shall adore in this place when I, the true Paschal Lamb, have been immolated. A new era, a new sacrifice is now about to begin and it shall last until the end of the world."

They then proceeded to the Paschal hearth at the end of the hall where formerly the Ark of the Covenant rested. There they found a fire already lit. Jesus sprinkled the hearth with blood and consecrated it as an altar. The rest of the blood, along with the fat, was thrown into the fire under the altar after which, followed by the apostles, Jesus walked around the Cenacle singing psalms and consecrated it as a new temple.

Meanwhile, Simeon's son had prepared the lamb. It was fixed upon a spit, the four legs fastened to a crosspiece and the hind ones to the spit. It looked so much like Jesus on the Cross! It was then, along with the three others that had been slaughtered in the Temple, that it was placed in the oven to be roasted. All the Paschal lambs of the Jews were immolated in the forecourt of the Temple in one or three different places according as to whether their owners were rich, poor or strangers. That of Jesus was not slaughtered in the Temple although he observed all the other points of the law most strictly. But that special lamb was only a figurehead. Jesus himself would on the next day become the true Paschal Lamb.

Jesus next gave the apostles an instruction about the Paschal lamb and the fulfillment of what it symbolized, and as the time was drawing near and Judas had returned, they began to prepare the tables. After that they put on the clothing of ceremony, which were in the anteroom, and they changed their shoes. Thus attired, each set went to their own table. The apostles went to the Cenacle proper. Each took a staff in hand and they walked in pairs to the table at which each stood in his place, his arms raised and the staff resting upon one.

Jesus stood in the centre of the table. He had two small staves that the master of the feast had presented to him. They were somewhat crooked on top and looked like short shepherd staves. It was a most touching sight to see Jesus leaning on these staves as he moved. It was as if he had the Cross, whose weight he would soon take upon his shoulders, now supporting him under the arms. Meanwhile, all were chanting: "Blessed be the Lord God of Israel," "Praise be the Lord," et cetera. When the prayer was ended, Jesus gave one of the staves to Peter, the other to John. They put them aside and passed them from hand to hand among the other apostles.

The table was narrow and only high enough to reach a half foot above the knee of a man standing by it. In form it was like a horseshoe and opposite Jesus, in the inner part of the half-circle, there was a space left free for the serving of the dishes. John and James the Greater and James the Less stood on Jesus' right, then came Bartholomew, still on the right but more toward the narrow end of the table, and around the corner at the inner sides stood Thomas and next to him Judas Iscariot. On Jesus' left were Peter, Andrew and Thaddeus, then as on the opposite side, there was Simon and around at the inner side, Matthew and Phillip.

In the centre of the table lay the Paschal lamb on a dish and all around the edge of the dish were little bunches of garlic. Nearby was another dish with the Paschal roasted meat and on either side was a plate of green herbs. These latter were arranged in an upright position and so closely together that they looked as if they were growing. There was another plate with little bunches of bitter herbs that looked like aromatic herbs. Directly in front of Jesus' place stood a bowl of yellowish-green herbs and another with some kind of brownish sauce. Small round loaves served the guests for plates and they made use of bone knives.

After the prayer, the master of the feast laid on the table in front of Jesus the knife for carving the roasted Paschal lamb, placed a cup of wine before him and from a jug filled six other cups, each of which he set between the apostles. Jesus blessed the wine and drank while the apostles drank two by two from one cup. Jesus then cut up the Paschal lamb. The apostles in turn reached for their little loaves on some kind of an instrument that held them fast and received each one a share. They ate it in haste, separating the flesh from the bones with their ivory knives and the bones were afterwards burned. They ate also, and that very quickly, the garlic and green herbs, first dipping them into the sauce. They then ate the Paschal lamb standing, leaning a little on the back of the seats. Jesus then broke one of the loaves of unleavened bread, covered up one part of it and divided the other among the apostles. After that they ate the little loaves and another cup of wine was brought. Jesus gave thanks but did not drink of it. He then said: "Take this wine and divide it among you for you shall henceforth drink no more wine until the kingdom of God comes."

After the apostles had drunk, two by two, they chanted while Jesus prayed. They again washed their hands and then reclined on the seats. During the preceding ceremony they had been standing, or at least supported themselves somehow, and everything was done in haste. Jesus also cut up another lamb, which was carried to the holy women at the side building where they were taking their meal. He became extremely serene and collected, more so than I had ever seen him and he bade the apostles to forget their cares. In the other room the Blessed Virgin was bright and cheerful as she sat at the table with the holy women and it was very touching to see her turning so gently to the other women when at times they approached her and drew her attention to them by a little pull of her veil.

While the apostles were eating the herbs, Jesus continued to converse with them still quite lovingly but he afterwards became grave and sad and said: "One among you will betray me — one whose hand is with me in the dish." He was at that moment distributing one of the vegetables, namely, the lettuce for which there was only one dish. He was passing it down his own side of the table and had directed Judas, who was sitting across from him, to distribute it on the other side. As Jesus made mention of a traitor, the apostles became very alarmed. Then he continued: "One whose hand is at me at table or whose hand dips with me in the dish," which is as much as to say: "One of the twelve who is eating and drinking with me — one with whom I am breaking my bread."

By these words, Jesus did not betray Judas to the others for "to dip into the same dish" was a common expression significant of the most intimate friendship. Still Jesus intended by it to warn Judas for he was really dipping his hand with him into the dish while distributing the lettuce. Later on, Jesus said: "The Son of Man indeed goes as it is written of him, but woe to that man to whom the Son of Man shall be betrayed! It were better for him if he had never been born." At these words the apostles became very much troubled for they did not understand him fully and they all asked in turn: "Lord, is it I?" Peter meanwhile, leaning behind Jesus towards John, motioned to him to ask the Lord who it was, for having often received reproofs from Jesus, he was anxious lest it might be himself. John at that time was reclining at Jesus' right and as all were leaning on their left arm in order to eat with the right hand.

At the request from Peter, John approached his head toward Jesus' breast and asked: "Lord, who is it?" It seemed to me that he was interiorly informed that Jesus was referring to Judas. John also understood it to be so when Jesus, having dipped into the sauce the morsel of bread folded in lettuce, offered it affectionately to Judas, who too was asking: "Lord, is it I?" Jesus looked at him lovingly and answered in general terms. To give bread dipped was a mark of love and confidence and Jesus did it with heartfelt love to warn Judas and to warn off the suspicions of the others. But Judas was interiorly inflamed with rage. However, I did not see John repeating to Peter what he had learned from Jesus although I saw him setting Peter's own mind at rest by a certain reassuring glance.

Then Jesus, while standing in the midst of the apostles, spoke to them quite solemnly for a long time. I remember that he spoke of his Kingdom, of going to his Father and he told them that before leaving them, he would give over to them all that he possessed. Then he gave them instructions about penance and knowledge about confession of sin, contrition and justice. I felt that this bore some reference to the washing of the feet and I saw that all, with the exception of Judas, acknowledged their sins with sorrow. This discourse was long and solemn. When it was over, Jesus, John and James the Less instructed some disciples to bring water from the anteroom and directed the others to place the seats in a half-circle. Meanwhile, Jesus himself retired to the anteroom to lay aside his mantle, gird on his robe and tied around himself a towel, one end of which he allowed to hang.

While these preparations were being made, the apostles got into some dispute as to whom among them should have the first place in the kingdom for as the Lord had announced that he was about to leave them and that his kingdom was at hand, they were strengthened and had an idea that he had a secret force somewhere which had been hidden and that he would achieve some earthly triumph at the very last moment. Meanwhile, Jesus, still in the anteroom, instructed John to take a basin and James the Less a leather bottle of water. The latter carried the bottle in front of his chest and after he had poured some water from the bottle into the basin, Jesus bade the two to follow him into the hall in the centre of which the master of the feast had set another large, empty basin.

Entering the hall in this order, Jesus in a few words reproved the apostles for the dispute that had arisen among them. He said, among other things, that he himself was their servant and that they should take their places on the seats for him to wash their feet. The apostles obeyed, observing the same order as at the table. They sat on the backs of their seats which were arranged in a half-circle and rested their naked feet upon the seat itself. Jesus went from one to the other and from the basin, held under them by John, he scooped up water over the feet presented to him and washed them. Then taking into his both hands the long end of the towel in which he was girded, he passed it over the feet to dry them and moved on with James to the next. John emptied the water after each one into the large basin in the centre of the room and then he turned to Jesus with the empty one. Then Jesus again poured water from the bottle held by James over the feet of the next apostle, and so on.

As it was during the whole of the Paschal supper, Jesus' demeanor was most touching and gracious and at this humble washing of his apostles' feet, he was ever so full of love. He did not perform it as if it were a mere ceremony but like a sacred act of love streaming straight from the heart. By it he wanted to give expression to the love that burned within him. When he came to Peter, the latter, through humility, objected and said: "Now, Lord, will you wash my feet?" And Jesus answered: "What I do you do not know now, but you shall know hereafter," and it appeared to me that he said to him in private: "Simon, you have deserved that my Father should reveal to you who I am, whence I came and wither I go. You alone have known and confessed it, therefore, I will build my Church upon you and the gates of hell shall not prevail against it. My power shall continue with your successors till the end of the world." Then Jesus pointed to Peter while saying to the others: "Peter shall be my representative when I shall go among you. He shall direct you and make known to you your mission." Peter, however, in his zeal looked upon it as too great a humiliation for his Master and said: "Never shall you wash my feet!" Jesus replied: "If I do not wash you, you shall have no part of me!" Thereupon Peter exclaimed: "Lord, wash me, not only my feet, but also my hands and my head!" To which Jesus replied: "He that is washed needs not but to wash his feet but is clean wholly. And you are clean, but not all." At these last words, Jesus was thinking of Judas.

During his instructions, Jesus had spoken of the washing of the feet as of a purification from daily falls because the feet, coming in continual contact with the earth in walking, are constantly liable to become soiled. In other words, this was a spiritual foot-washing, a kind of absolution. When Jesus washed Judas' feet, it was in a most touching and loving manner. He pressed them to his cheek and in a low tone bade him enter into himself for he had been unfaithful and a traitor for the past year. But Judas appeared not to notice and addressed some words to John. This aroused Peter's anger and he exclaimed: "Judas, the Master is speaking to you!" Then Judas made some vague and evasive remark, such as: "Lord, far be it from me!"

Jesus' words to Judas had passed unremarked by the other apostles for he deliberately spoke softly and they did not hear. They were moreover busy putting on their sandals. Judas' treachery caused Jesus much pain. Jesus next delivered a sermon on humility. He told them that he who was the greatest among them should be the servant and that in the future they should in humility wash one another's feet. Many other things he said bearing reference to their dispute as to who should be the greatest, as is recorded in the Gospel. Jesus now put on the garments that he had laid aside and the apostles let down theirs that had been girded up for the eating of the Paschal lamb.

Again Jesus prayed and taught, his words glowing with fire and love. He then took the plate with the morsels of bread and said: "Take this and eat. This is my body which will be given up for you." While saying these words, he stretched forth his hand over it, as if giving a blessing, and as he did so, a brilliant light emanated from him. His words were luminous as also was the bread, which appeared as a body of light and entered the body of the apostles. It was as if Jesus himself flowed into them. I saw all of them penetrated with life and bathed in light. Judas alone was in darkness.

Jesus had presented the bread first to Peter, then to John and next made a sign to Judas, who was sitting diagonally from him, to approach. Judas was the third to whom Jesus presented the Blessed Sacrament but it seemed as if his words turned back from the mouth of the traitor. Jesus then said to Judas: "What you are about to do, do it quickly." Then the Lord administered the bread to the rest of the apostles, who came up two by two, each one holding in front of his neighbour a little stiff cover with an ornamental edge that had lain over the chalice.

Jesus next raised the chalice by its two handles to the level of his face and pronounced the words of consecration. "Take this and drink. This is the cup of my blood, the blood of the new and everlasting covenant. It will be shed for you and for all so that sins will be forgiven." While doing so, he was wholly transfigured and, as it were, transparent. He called Peter and John to drink from the chalice while yet it was in his hands and then he set it down. With a little spoon, John removed some of the wine from the chalice into small cups, which Peter handed to the apostles, who, two by two, drank from the same cup. Judas also (although of this I am not quite certain) partook of the chalice but he did not return to his

place for he immediately left the Cenacle without the prayer of thanksgiving. The others thought that Jesus had given him some commission to execute. Christ therefore celebrated the Passover according to the historic Hebrew rite coming down from the patriarchal days of Moses and the prophets but changed it into the Christian Mass. On that night he performed his last major miracle on earth. This time he changed wine into his precious blood and bread into his sacred body.

The rest of the wine which was in the chalice, Jesus poured into a small cup, then holding his finger over the chalice, he bade Peter and John to pour wine upon them. This ablution he gave to them to drink from the chalice and pouring what remained into smaller cups, he passed it down to the rest of the apostles. After that he wiped the chalice and put into it the little cup with what was left.

It was to be the fulfillment of Psalm 40 and Paul's sermon to the Hebrews: "Bulls' blood and goats' blood are useless for taking away sins and this is what he said on coming into the world: 'You who wanted no sacrifice or oblation, prepared a body for me. You took no pleasure in holocausts or sacrifices for sin; then I said, just as was written of me in the scroll of the book: 'God, here I am. I am coming to do your will'" (Hebrews 10:5–7).

Jesus then gave to the apostles an instruction full of mystery. He told them how they were to preserve the Blessed Sacrament in memory of him until the end of the world, taught them the necessary formats for making use of and communicating it and in what manner they were to teach and publish the mystery. He again delivered a long instruction and prayed several times with deep emotion. He appeared as if conversing with his heavenly Father and to be overflowing with love and enthusiasm. He addressed some words in private to Peter and John, who were sitting next to him, in reference to some of his earlier instructions. They were to communicate them to the other apostles and these in turn to the disciples and holy women, according to the capacity of each for such knowledge. He spoke for some time to John alone. Of this I only remember that Jesus told him that his life would be longer than that of the others and that he said something about seven churches, something about crowns and angels and similar significant symbols by which he designated certain epochs. The other apostles seemed to be slightly jealous over this special communication with John.

He alluded several times to his traitor, saying: "Now he is doing this, now he is doing that," and as he spoke, I saw Judas doing just what he said. When Peter protested that he would certainly remain faithful to him, Jesus said to him: "Simon, Simon! Behold Satan has desired to have you that he may sift you as wheat, but I have prayed for you that your faith fail not and you, being once converted, confirm your brethren." Jesus also said that wither he was going, they could not follow, Peter again exclaimed that he would follow him even unto death. Whereupon Jesus replied to him: "Amen, amen, I say to you, before the cock crows twice, you will deny me thrice!" Then Jesus said: "It is enough. Let us go hence!" Afterwards they recited the hymn of thanksgiving, put aside the table and went into the anteroom. Here Jesus met his mother, Mary Cleophas and Mary Magdalene, who all besought him imploringly not to go to the Mount of Olives for it was reported that he would there be arrested. Jesus comforted them in a few words and set out quickly past them. It was then about nine o' clock. They went in haste down the road and directed their steps towards Mount Olivet.

When Jesus left the Cenacle with the eleven, his soul was very troubled and his sadness on the increase. He led the eleven to the Mount of Olives by an unfrequented path through the Valley of Josaphat. While walking in the valley with the apostles, Jesus said that he would one day return hither but not poor and powerless as he then was, to judge the world. Then men, he said, trembling will cry out: "Now, mountains, cover us!" But the disciples did not understand him. They thought that he was suffering from weakness and exhaustion and was wandering in speech. The apostles were still full of enthusiasm and devotion, inspired by the reception of the Most Holy Sacrament and the loving, solemn discourses of Jesus. Afterwards, they crowded eagerly around him and expressed their love in different ways, protesting that they never could, and would, abandon him.

Catherine Emmerich went into greater detail, however, the following day, the sacrifice of Isaac was renewed on Calvary. But whereas on the Mount of Moriah God supplied the victim (a ram) to be substituted for Isaac and spared both the life of the son and the hearts of his father Abraham and his mother Sarah, on Calvary God fully accepted both the sacrifice of his son and the broken heart of his mother, Mary, the second Eve, the ewe who witnessed her lamb slaughtered as she stood helplessly by.

Now let us read parts of what she wrote about the agony in the Garden of Gethsemane and onwards.

Chapter 6

The Agony in the Garden

It was about 9 o' clock when Jesus reached Gethsemane with the disciples. Darkness had fallen upon the earth but the moon was lighting up the sky. Jesus was very sad. He bade eight of them to remain in the garden where there was a kind of summerhouse built of branches and foliage. He took Peter, John and James the Greater with him, crossed the road and went on for a few minutes until he reached the Garden of Olives further up the mountain. He was impressibly sad. John asked how he, who had always consoled them, could now be so dejected. He replied: "My soul is sorrowful even unto death."

He glanced around and on all sides saw anguish and temptation gathering about him like dense clouds filled with frightful pictures. It was at that moment he said to the three apostles: "Remain here and watch with me. Pray lest you enter into temptation!" Jesus went a few steps forward and crunched down into a grotto formed by an overhanging rock. It was about six feet deep, and shrubs hanging from the rocks towering over the entrance made it a place to which no eye could see. His sorrow and anguish increased. He withdrew tremblingly into the back of the cave like one seeking shelter from a violent tempest and there he prayed. It was as if that narrow cave encompassed the horrible, agonizing visions of all the sins with their delights committed from the fall of our first parents until the end of the world. He fell on his face, calling upon God in unspeakable sorrow and anguish.

He saw in countless forms all the sins of the world with an innate hideousness. This enormous mass of sin and iniquity passed before the soul of Jesus in an ocean of horrible visions and he offered himself as an expiatory sacrifice for all and implored that all their punishment and chastisement should fall upon him. He writhed like a worm under the weight of his sorrow and agony and his soul shrank in fright from the multitude and heinousness of man's sins and ingratitude against God. So overpowering was the sadness and the agony of heart which fell upon him, that, trembling and shuddering, he prayed imploringly: "Father, if it be possible, remove this chalice from me. My father, all things are possible to you. Take this chalice from me." Then recovering himself, he added: "But not what I will but what you will." Of course, his will and the Father's were one but now that through love he had delivered himself up to the weakness of his human nature, he shuddered at the thought of death.

Wringing his hands, he swayed from side to side and a sweat of agony covered him. He trembled and shuddered. He arose but his trembling knees could scarcely support him. His countenance was quite disfigured and almost unrecognizable. His lips were white and his hair stood on end. It was about half-past ten when he staggered to his feet, and bathed in sweat and often falling, tottered rather than walked to where the three disciples were awaiting him. Exhausted with fatigue, sorrow and anxiety, they had fallen asleep. Jesus went to them like a man overwhelmed with sorrow whom terror drives to the company of friends, but he found the apostles sleeping. He clasped his hands and, sinking down from grief and exhaustion, he said: "Simon, are you sleeping?" At these words they awoke. In his spiritual dereliction, he then said: "What! Could you not watch one hour with me?"

When they found him so terrified and disfigured, so pale, trembling and bathed with sweat, shivering and shaking, his voice feeble and stammering, they were altogether at a loss what to think. Had he not appeared surrounded by the light so well known to them, they would not have recognized him as Jesus. He exhorted them to pray lest they fell into temptation "for the spirit is willing but the flesh is weak." In his overpowering sorrow, he said many other things to them and remained with them for about a quarter of an hour. He then returned to the grotto where his anguish increased. The apostles, seeing him leave them, stretched out their hands after him, wept, threw themselves into one another's arms, and asked: "What does this all mean? What is the matter with him? He is so thoroughly desolate."

Covering their heads, they began in great anxiety to pray. However, the eight, who had remained at the entrance, did not sleep. The anxiety that hallmarked all of Jesus' last actions on that evening greatly disquieted them and they wandered around Mount Olivet seeking a hiding place for themselves. Indeed, his sorrow was such that a bloody sweat poured from the pores of his sacred body.

Jesus writhed in anguish and wrung his hands. As if overwhelmed, he fell repeatedly on his knees while so violent a struggle went on between his human will and his repugnance to suffer so much for so thankless a people. The sweat poured from him in a stream of heavy drops of blood to the ground and in his distress, he raised his voice for some instant in loud cries of anguish. I saw that the three apostles sprang up in fright. With raised hands, they listened to Jesus' cries and were on the point of hastening to him, but Peter stopped James and John, saying: "Stay here! I will go to him." I saw him hurrying forward and entering the grotto. "Master," he cried, "what has happened to you?" But he paused in terror at the sight of Jesus bathed in blood and trembling with fear. Jesus made no answer and appeared not to notice Peter.

Then Peter returned to the other two and reported that Jesus had only answered him with sighs and groans. This news increased the sorrow and anxiety of the apostles. They covered their heads and sat weeping and praying with many tears. He eventually spoke to his apostles in his deep affliction. On the morrow, he said, he is going to die. In another hour, his enemies would seize him, drag him before the courts of justice, abuse him, deride him, scourge him, and put him to death in a most horrible manner. He begged them to console his mother. He recounted to them in bitter anguish all that he would have to suffer until the evening of the next day and repeatedly begged them to comfort his mother and Magdalene. It was then a quarter past eleven.

During this agony of Jesus, I saw the Blessed Virgin overwhelmed with sorrow and anguish. She was with Mary Magdalene and Mary Marcus in a garden adjoining the house. She had sunk on her knees on a stone slab and was profoundly distracted interiorly, seeing only and feeling only the sufferings of her divine son. I saw her walking along, veiled, her arms outstretched toward the Mount of Olives where she saw the spirit of Jesus agonizing in sweat and blood. I saw that Jesus was also stirred with thoughts of her. He saw and felt also his blessed mother's sorrow and anguish of heart.

Chapter 7

The Arrest of Jesus

When he was arrested in the Garden of Olives, they bound him with the greatest crudeness and barbarous brutality. The Pharisees meanwhile uttered insolent and scornful words at him. They bound his hands upon his chest and in a cruel manner, with sharp new cords, they pitilessly fastened the wrist of the right hand to the left forearm just below the elbow and that of the left hand to the right forearm. They put around his waist a broad girdle studded with sharp points and bound his hands at the end with links of willow which were fixed to the girdle. Around his neck they laid a collar on which there were points and instruments to wound, and from it hung two straps, which like a stole, were crossed over the chest and bound down to the girdle so tightly that his neck was not free to move. At four points of this girdle were fastened long ropes by means of which the executioners could drag him hither and thither according to their wicked will. After several more torches had been lit, the pitiable procession was set in motion. Ten of the guards then followed the executioners, dragging Jesus by the ropes. Next came the scoffing of the Pharisees and ten other soldiers were at the rear of the procession.

The disciples were still straying about, wailing and lamenting as if bereft of their senses. John, however, was following the last of the guards rather closely behind. The Pharisees, seeing him, ordered him to be seized and at this command, some of the guards turned and hurried after him but he fled from them. They then led Jesus around the roughest roads, over rocks and stones and mire, keeping the long ropes stretched while they themselves sought better good pathways for themselves. In this way, Jesus had to go wherever their ropes would allow him. His tormentors carried in their hands knotted cords with which they struck him as a butcher might do the animal he was leading to slaughter, all this accompanied with mockery and insults so low and indecent that the repetition of them would be revolting. Jesus was barefoot and fell several times during this journey.

It was towards midnight when Jesus was led through the court-yard into the palace of Annas, his head bowed, his garments wet and spotted with mud, his hands fettered, his waist bound by ropes, the ends of which the archers held. Annas could scarcely wait for the arrival of poor Jesus. He was beaming with mischievous joy. He was president of a certain tribunal to examine false doctrines and to hand over the accused to the High Priest. Anne Catherine Emmerich wrote several pages describing the awful insults and treatment Jesus received at this tribunal as the Passion continued.

He was then led to Caiaphas and once more had to undergo further horrible mockeries and insults. At one stage Caiaphas, in-furiated by the wrangling of two witnesses, rose from his seat, went down a couple of steps to Jesus and said: "Will you answer nothing to the testimony against you?" He was annoyed that Jesus would not look at him. At this the bullies pulled Jesus' head back by the hair and with their fists cuffed him under his chin, but his glance was still downwards. Caiaphas angrily raised his hands and said in a tone full of rage: "I adjure you by the living God that you tell us whether you are Christ, the Messiah, the Son of the Most Blessed God." A solemn silence fell upon the clamoring crowd. Jesus then said in a voice inexpressibly majestic, a voice that struck awe into all hearts: "I am! You said it! And I say to you, soon you shall see the Son of Man sitting at the right hand of the power of God and coming in the clouds of heaven."

When Jesus solemnly declared that he was the Christ, the Son of God, it was as if all hell grew terror-stricken before him and as if it launched the whole force of its rage against him by means of those gathered in the tribunal of Caiaphas. Caiaphas, as if also in-spired by hell, seized him by his mantle, clipped it with a knife and with a whizzing noise, tore it as he exclaimed in a loud voice: "He has blasphemed. What need have we of further witnesses? Behold now you have heard the blasphemy. What do you think?" At these words, the whole assembly rose and cried out in a horrid voice: "He is guilty of death! He is guilty of death!" The High Priest then shouted: "Render to the blasphemer the honour which is due to him. I deliver this king to you." Meanwhile, John in his deep affection thought only of the Blessed Virgin. He feared that the dreadful news might be suddenly communicated to her by some enemy and so, casting at Jesus a glance that said: "Master, you know why I am going," he hurried from the Judgment Hall to seek the Blessed Virgin.

Now they exercised their villainy upon Jesus in a manner altogether frantic and irrational. They put upon him, one after the other, several crowns of straw and bark plaited in various ludicrous forms which, with wicked words of mockery, they afterwards struck off from his head. Sometimes they shouted: "Behold the Son of David crowned with the crown of his father!" They struck him with their fists and sticks, threw him from side to side and spat on him. They had already forcibly and painfully pulled and torn much of the hair of his beard and covered him with mud and spittle. They also passed a wet smeary rag over his face and shoulders as if cleansing him although in reality they were rendering him more filthy than before. Finally, they poured the whole contents of the basin over his face. This last outrage, though without their intending it, showed a likeness between Jesus and the Paschal lamb, for on this day the lambs to be slaughtered for sacrifice were first washed in the pond near the sheep gate and then in the Pool of Bethsaida to the south of the Temple.

But one will have to read the complete revelations of the mystic and be prepared to be shocked by the extreme degree of man's inhumanity to man and, above all, to the God-Man, the God who chose to become man in order to suffer for us and from us. He was then scourged at the instruction of Pilate, who was hoping that it would satisfy the blood-thirsty crowd.

Chapter 8

The Scourging at the Pillar

There were six scourgers, dark, swarthy men, all somewhat shorter than Jesus. Their loins were girded and the rest of their clothing consisted of a leather jacket open at the sides and covering the upper part of the body like a scapular. They were evil men from the frontiers of Egypt, who had been condemned for their crimes to hard labour and were employed in erecting public buildings, the most criminal being selected to act as executioners in the praetorium. These barbarous men had scourged poor criminals to death many times at this same pillar. They resembled wild beasts or demons and appeared to be half drunk. Although he followed without offering the least resistance, they struck Our Lord with their fists and dragged him by the cords to the pillar to which he was pinioned. Then they barbarously knocked him down against the pillar.

This pillar stood alone in centre of the court and did not serve to sustain any part of the building. It was not very high for a tall man could touch the top by stretching out his arms. There was a large iron ring at the top. It is quite impossible to describe the cruelty and barbarity shown by these ruffians towards Jesus during that short walk to the pillar. They tore off the mantle with which he had been clothed at the court of Herod and almost threw him to the ground. Jesus trembled and shuddered before the pillar and took off his garments as quickly as he could but his hands were bloody and swollen. He prayed ever so touchingly and, for an instant, turned his face towards his most afflicted mother, who was standing overcome with grief with the holy women in a corner of one of the porches around the square not far from the scourging place. This look of his quite unnerved her. She fainted and would have fallen had not the holy women who were there supported her.

Jesus put his arms around the pillar and when his hands were thus raised, the scourgers fastened them to the iron ring which was at the top of the pillar. They then pulled his arms to its height. In so doing, they stretched his whole body so that his feet, tightly bound at the base, barely touched the ground. Jesus writhed like a worm under the brutal whipping of these barbarians. They resounded through the air, forming a kind of touching accompaniment to the hissing of the instruments of torture and his deep groans could be heard from afar. The clamour of the Pharisees and the people formed another kind of accompaniment, which at times deadened and smothered his sacred and mournful cries.

Meanwhile, Pilate continued parleying and negotiating with the people and when he demanded silence in order to be able to speak, at such moments you might again hear the noise of the scourges, the moans of Jesus, the imprecations of the soldiers and the bleating of the Paschal lambs which were being washed in the pool near the sheep gate. There was something peculiarly touching about the plaintive bleating of these lambs as they alone appeared to unite their lamentations with the suffering moans of the true Lamb of God.

The two ruffians continued to strike him with unremitting violence for a quarter of an hour and were then succeeded by two others. Jesus' body was entirely covered with black, blue and red marks. His sacred blood was trickling down on the ground. He trembled and shuddered and yet furious cries issued from the assembled crowds who showed that their cruelty was far from being satiated. A second pair of executioners then commenced scourging Jesus with the greatest possible fury. They made use of different kind of rough rods, set with thorns and covered with knots and splinters. This time the blows from these sticks tore his flesh to pieces and his blood spouted out so that the arms of the scourgers were sprinkled with it. Jesus moaned and prayed and shuddered in his agony.

Two new executioners took the places of the last mentioned, who were beginning to flag. Their scourging instruments were composed of small chains or straps covered with iron hooks, which penetrated to the bone and tore off large pieces of flesh at every blow. O, who can describe the awful barbarity of that spectacle! They untied Jesus turned him around and again fastened him this time with his back toward the pillar. As he was totally unable to support himself in an upright position, they passed cords around his waist, under his arms and above his knees, and having once more bound his hands tightly into the rings which were placed at the upper part of the pillar, they recommenced scourging him with even greater fury than before and one among them struck him constantly on the face with a rod.

By now the body of Our Lord was perfectly torn to shreds. It was but one huge wound. He looked at his torturers with eyes filled with blood as if entreating mercy, but their brutality appeared to increase and each moment his moans became more and more feeble. The dreadful scourging had been continued without intermission for three quarters of an hour. During these forty-five minutes the Blessed Virgin witnessed the scourging of her divine son. I saw her in her uninterrupted ecstasy during the time of the scourging of her divine Son. She saw and suffered with inexpressible love and grief all the torments he was enduring. She groaned feebly and her eyes were red with weeping. She wore a long blue robe partly covered by a cloak made of white wool and her veil was of creamy-white. At the termination of the scourging, she came to herself for a time and saw her divine son torn and mangled, being led away by his torturers after the scourging. With his garment he wiped his eyes which were filled with blood so that he might see his mother. It was heart-breaking to see her stretch out her hands towards him in agony.

When the cords that bound Jesus were eventually cut, he sank, covered with blood at the foot of the pillar and lay unconscious in his own blood. The executioners then left him lying there and went to drink while their villainous companions were weaving the crown of thorns. The executioners again returned, and kicking Jesus with their feet, forced him to rise for they had not yet finished with him. They struck him while he crawled after his linen girdle, which the wicked wretches kicked away with shouts of derision from side to side so that like a worm he had to crawl around the ground in his own blood in order to reach his girdle and with it cover his severely lacerated loins.

When he was driven into the praetorium after the scourging to submit to the crowning with thorns, he wiped the blood from his eyes in order to see his afflicted mother again. As he passed, she lifted her hands again towards him in agony and gazed after him and his blood-stained footsteps.

Chapter 9

The Agony of the Mother

By special favour of the Lord, the Blessed Virgin was able to see in visions everything that happened to her divine son during his Passion. Thus she was able to co-operate with him in his redeeming suffering for mankind by uniting the prayers and sacrifices of her Immaculate Heart to those of his Sacred Heart. Indeed, throughout his Passion, Our Lord derived most of his consolation from the love and holiness of his mother.

When the Saviour and his apostles left the Cenacle after the Last Supper for Gethsemane, the Blessed Virgin went to the home of Mary Mark with Magdalene and several of the holy women. On the way they met Lazarus, Nicodemus and Joseph of Arimathea, who reported that they knew of no immediate steps being planned against Jesus but Mary described to them Judas' sudden departure from the Cenacle and she expressed her fear that he intended to betray Jesus that same night. Actually, she had witnessed in a vision the plotting of Judas and the Pharisees.

As Jesus began to pray in the Garden of Gethsemane that night, his mother likewise retired to a private room and begged the Eternal Father that she might be allowed to feel all the physical and spiritual pain and torture which her Son was about to undergo. The Holy Trinity granted her prayer. Indeed, when the soldiers arrested and bound Jesus, she also felt on her wrists the same pains caused by the ropes and chains on his flesh. Similarly, she felt on her delicate body all the blows and kicks and falls which he suffered while being dragged to the palace of the High Priest.

The Blessed Virgin went out into the dark streets with some friends as they wanted to find out what was going to be done to Jesus. They were then able to watch the procession of the guards and their victim from a distance. Mary was speechless with grief. Meanwhile, the little group of holy women tried to avoid the crowds that were gathering and they were often obliged to hide in an alley

when a band of Jesus' enemies passed by. In fact, several times
Mary and her friends endured insults from women of loose character, and more than once they heard men curse or slander her son.
They therefore led his mother along unfrequented routes in order
to shun those by which Jesus was being dragged and so spare her
the anguish of meeting him. What a sad sight it was to see the
mother pierced with such anguish and hurrying through the streets
at midnight with the holy women from one friend's house to another, their hearts beating with fear at being out at so unusual an
hour! More than once they heard bitter, malicious remarks against
her son and rarely a compassionate word.

Then the holy women went to the home of Lazarus' sister,
Martha, in the western part of the city where John met them and
told them all that had happened since Jesus had left the Cenacle.
They were deeply upset and each tried to help and console one
another. At intervals other messengers came and knocked lightly at
the door, bringing further discouraging news.

Mary Magdalene, who was almost out of her mind with grief,
staggered with the others through the moonlit streets, sobbing and
wringing her hands. Again they were frequently insulted by the
enemies of Jesus. The Blessed Virgin endured this all in silence
like her divine son, who at the same moment was being mocked
and struck in the High Priest's palace, but her inner suffering in
sympathy in him was so intense that occasionally her companions
had to support her in their arms. Once, however, when they met a
friendly group, who greeted Mary as "the most unhappy and afflicted mother of the Holy One of Israel," the Blessed Virgin thanked
them earnestly for their kindness.

Near the palace of Caiaphas they had to pass by a yard where
some cursing labourers were hammering away at the Cross for the
newly condemned criminal. Eventually she was led by John to a
spot where she could hear the sighs of Jesus and the insults and
blows which he was enduring. However, some men in the crowd
coming out of the palace recognized her and exclaimed loudly:
"Isn't that the Galilean's mother? Her son will certainly be crucified, but not until after the festival--unless he is really the greatest
of criminals!"

As Jesus was dragged to a filthy underground prison cell to spend the hours until dawn, Mary and the holy women sadly returned to Martha's home. After sunrise, the next morning, Caiphas sent Jesus to Pilate but although John warned the Blessed Virgin that it would break her heart to see her Son after he had been so defiled and disfigured as to be nearly unrecognizable, Mary took her mantle and veil and said solemnly: "Let us follow my son to Pilate. My eyes must see him again." But in the crowded streets, she had to listen repeatedly to the cruel comments of hard-hearted people concerning the guilt and fate of her son. Then suddenly at a sharp turn in the street she came upon the procession. At last she saw Jesus again. But now he was staggering along, bound and chained, covered with bruises and saliva, constantly being jerked forward by the ropes which his merciless guards held, but through it all he remained a meek and silent victim, humbly submitting to a storm of inhumane mockery, curses and insults.

For a second, so unrecognizable was he, Mary was so utterly shocked that she gasped: "Is this my Son? O Jesus, my Jesus!" Then she suddenly prostrated herself on the ground in reparation to his desecrated divinity. When he passed close by her, mother and son exchanged a brief look charged with such an indescribably great and heart-rending mutual love and compassion. Following bravely after Jesus, Mary came to the palace of Pilate and from the corner of the forum, she witnessed the first Roman trial. As she saw with what furious hatred the enemies of Christ attacked him and mercilessly sought his death, she held her mantle before her face and quietly, in the ultimate and extreme anguish of a mother whose love knew no bounds, wept tears of blood.

When he was again brought before Pilate, the holy women heard a rumour that the Roman governor was trying to release Jesus. Trembling and shivering with all the hopes and fears of a mother, Mary's heart was cruelly torn between her natural desire for her son's safety and her supernatural submission to the word of God. But Pilate soon weakly yielded to the fury of the enemies of Jesus by freeing Barabbas and condemning the Galilean to be scourged.

As the innocent victim was being stripped and attached to a pillar, for an instant he turned his head towards his mother, who was standing with the holy women not far from the scourging place. It seemed as though he was trying to say to her: "O mother, turn your eyes away from me!" At this point Mary fainted in the arms of her companions and had to be led away. It was nine o'clock in the morning when the scourging was over. I saw the Blessed Virgin and Magdalene approach the place of the scourging. They cast themselves on their knees and soaked up the sacred blood of Jesus with a cloth until not a trace of it could be found.

Chapter 10

The Crowning with Thorns and His Condemnation

In the middle of the court there stood a fragment of a pillar and on it was placed a very low stool which these cruel men maliciously covered with sharp stones and bits of broken potsherds. They then tore off the garment of Jesus thereby reopening all his wounds, threw over his shoulders an old scarlet mantle which barely reached his knees, dragged him to the seat prepared, and violently pushed him down upon it, having first placed a crown of thorns upon his head. The crown of thorns was made of three branches plaited together, the largest part of the thorns being purposely turned inwards so as to pierce his head. Having first placed these twisted branches on his forehead, they tied them tightly together at the back of his head and no sooner was this accomplished to their satisfaction than they put a large reed into his hand, doing all with derisive levity as if they were really crowning him king. They then snatched the reed from his hand and struck his head so violently with it that his eyes were filled with blood.

They knelt before him, they ridiculed him, stuck out their tongue at him, spat in his face, and buffeted him, saying at the same time: "Hail, King of the Jews!" Then they threw down the stool with the sharp stones and potsherds, pulled him up again from the ground and painfully reseated him with the greatest possible force. This shameful scene was protracted a full half-hour and during the whole time the Roman soldiers continued to applaud and encourage the perpetration of still greater outrages.

The cruel executioners then re-led Jesus to Pilate's palace, with a scarlet cloak thrown over his shoulders, the crown of thorns on his head and the reed in his fettered hand. He was thoroughly unrecognizable, his eyes, mouth and beard being covered with blood, his body but one raw wound and his back bowed down as that of an aged man while every limb trembled as he walked. When Pilate saw him standing at the entrance of his tribunal, even he was startled with compassion whilst the barbarous priests and the people, far from being moved to pity, continued their insults and mockery.

When Jesus was ascending the stairs, Pilate came forward and the trumpet was sounded to announce that the governor was about to speak. He addressed the Chief Priests and the bystanders: "Behold, I bring him forth to you that you may know that I find no cause in him." The scourgers then led Jesus up to Pilate so that the people might again feast their cruel eyes on him and the state of degradation into which he was reduced. Terrible and heart-rending, indeed, was the spectacle he presented, and an exclamation of horror burst forth from the multitude followed by a dead silence when he, with difficulty, raised his wounded head, crowned as it was with thorns, and cast his exhausted glance, on the excited throng. Pilate then exclaimed, as he pointed him to the people: "*Ecce homo!*" ("*Behold the man!*") But the hatred of the High Priests and their followers was, as if possible, increased at the sight of Jesus and they cried out repeatedly: "Crucify him!" Meanwhile Jesus, the scarlet cloak of derision thrown upon his lacerated body, his pierced head sinking under the weight of the thorny crown, his fettered hands holding the mock scepter, was standing thus before Pilate like a helpless lamb.

Pilate then sounded the trumpet to demand silence and said: "Take you him and crucify him for I find no cause in him." "We have a law, and according to that law he ought to die," replied the priests, "because he made himself the Son of God." These words revived the fears of Pilate. He took Jesus into another room and asked him: "Who are you?" But Jesus made no answer. "Speak you not to me?" said Pilate. "Do you not know that I have power to crucify you and power to release you?" "You should not have any power against me," replied Jesus, "unless it were given to you from above. Therefore he who has delivered me to you has the greater sin."

Pilate was half-frightened but at the same time also half-angry at the words of Jesus. He returned to the balcony and again declared that he would release Jesus. But they cried out: "If you release this man, you are not Caesar's friend. For whomsoever makes himself a king speaks against Caesar" and the cry: "Crucify him! Crucify him!" resounded on all sides. Pilate then took water and washed his hands before the people, saying: "I am innocent of the blood of this just man. Look you to it." A frightful and unanimous cry then came from the dense multitude, who assembled from all parts of Palestine: "His blood be upon us and upon our children," they cried. This iniquitous sentence against the innocent lamb was given at about ten o clock in the morning.

On hearing this, Mary, the mother of Jesus, became unconscious for a few moments as she was now certain that her beloved son must die the most ignominious and the most painful of all deaths. John and the holy women then carried her away to prevent the heartless beings who surrounded them from adding crime to crime by jeering at her grief. But no sooner did she revive a little than she begged to be taken again to each spot which had been sanctified by the sufferings and blood of her son in order to bedew them with her tears.

Chapter 11

The Way of the Cross

When, after the crowning with thorns, which the Blessed Virgin again saw in vision, Jesus was once more brought before the people and Pilate had exclaimed: "Behold the man!" ("Ecce Homo!"), Mary was then seen to fall onto her knees and worshiped her Lord while his enemies shouted: "Crucify him! Crucify him!"

Jesus was then led into the middle of the court and the slaves threw down the Cross at his feet. He knelt down by its side, encircled it with his sacred arms and kissed it three times, addressing at the same time a most touching prayer of thanksgiving to his heavenly Father for the work of redemption which had been entrusted to him. And so, just as it was a custom among the pagans for the priests to embrace a new altar, Jesus, in like manner, embraced his Cross, that august altar on which the bloody and expiatory sacrifice was about to be offered.

The executioners placed the heavy Cross on his right shoulder, while supporting its great weight with his hand. They then pulled him roughly up for he was totally unable to arise without assistance and he then felt upon his shoulders the weight of that wood. Thus began the march of the "King of Kings". By means of ropes, which they had fastened to the foot of the Cross, two soldiers supported it to prevent it getting entangled in anything on the roads and four other soldiers took hold of the ropes which they had fastened to Jesus beneath his clothes. The sight of Jesus trembling under his burden strongly reminded me of Isaac when he carried the wood destined for his own sacrifice up the mountain.

The afflicted mother of Jesus had left the forum, accompanied by John and some other women. Immediately after the unjust sentence was pronounced, she had begged John to take her to some place through which he must pass. John asked and obtained leave from a kind-hearted servant to stand at an entrance place with Mary and her companions. Closely wrapped in a cloak of bluish-gray colour, she was pale and her eyes were red with weeping. After praying fervently, she turned to John and said: "Should I remain? Ought I to go away? Shall I have the strength to support such a sight?" But John answered: "If you do not remain to see him pass you will grieve forever afterwards." The Blessed Virgin then begged John to take her to some place where her son would pass. They therefore waited at the entrance of a certain large house on the way.

I beheld him with his bare feet swollen and bleeding, his back bent as though he were about to sink under the heavy weight of the Cross, and his whole body was covered with wounds and blood. He appeared to be half fainting from exhaustion, weak from the loss of blood, and thoroughly parched with thirst produced by dehydration, fever and pain. Yet he supported the Cross on his right shoulder with his right hand and the left hand hung almost powerless at his side. The four men, who held the cords which were fastened around his waist, walked at some distance from him. The two who were in front pulled him on and the two behind dragged him back so that he could not move on at all without the greatest difficulty.

His hands were cut by the cords with which they had been bound, his face bloody and disfigured, his hair and beard saturated with clotted blood. The weight of the Cross and of his chains combined to press upon and make the woolen robe cleave to his wounds and reopen them. Derisive and heartless words were addressed to him but he continued to pray for his persecutors and his face bore an expression of combined love and resignation.

When those who were carrying the instruments for the execution were approaching and the mother of Jesus saw their insolent and triumphant looks, she could not control her emotions but joined her hands as if to implore the help of heaven, whereupon one among them said to his companions: "What woman is that who is uttering such lamentations?" Another answered: "She is the mother of the Galilean." When the cruel men heard this, far from being moved to compassion, they began to make game of the grief of this most afflicted mother. They pointed at her and one of them took the nails which were to be used for fastening Jesus to the Cross and showed them to her in a most insulting and taunting manner. But she quickly turned away, fixed her eyes upon Jesus, who was drawing near, and leaned against a pillar for support where she should faint from grief.

Then came her beloved son. He was almost sinking under the heavy weight of his Cross, and his head, still crowned with thorns, was drooping in agony on his shoulder. He cast a look of compassion and sorrow upon his mother, staggered and fell upon his hands and knees for the second time. Mary was thoroughly agonized at this sight. Springing from the doorway into the midst of the group, who were insulting and abusing him, she threw herself on her knees by his side and embraced him. The only words of anguish I heard were: "Son!" and "Mother!"

A momentary confusion ensued. John and the holy women tried to raise Mary from the ground and the executioners reproached her, one of them saying: "What have you to do here, woman? He would not have been in our hands if he had been better brought up." However, a few of the soldiers looked touched and although they obliged the Blessed Virgin to retire to the doorway, not one laid hands upon her. John and the holy women then surrounded her as she fell half-fainting against a stone which was near the doorway. As Jesus staggered on toward Calvary, Mary fell half-fainting against a wall near the doorway, and two disciples carried her inside the house. After the procession had passed, Mary and John and their friends followed it along the sorrowful way to Calvary.

Jesus stumbled against a large stone and the Cross slipped from his shoulder. He fell upon a stone and was totally unable to rise. The crowd howled with joy at each fall. He now walks bending and this hampers his steps. He stumbles again and falls on both knees hurting himself where he was already wounded. One can clearly see on his right shoulder the wound made by the rubbing of the Cross, which has opened the many sores of the scourges, making them all into one from which serum and blood transude so that the spot on his white tunic is all stained. "Make sure that he dies only on the Cross," shouted the crowd. This fall caused a new delay to Calvary as he could not stand up again, whereupon the Pharisees shouted to the soldiers: "We shall never get him to the place of execution alive if you do not find someone to carry his Cross." At that moment, Simon of Cyrene, a pagan, happened to pass by, accompanied by his three children. The soldiers, perceiving by his dress that he was a pagan, seized him and ordered him to assist Jesus in carrying his Cross.

Now, the Blessed Virgin was carried away fainting after this sad meeting with her son loaded with his Cross but she soon recovered consciousness and accompanied by her companions, she went to the house of Lazarus which was at the bottom of the town and where Martha, Magdalene and many holy women were already assembled. Mary and the other holy women then set off together towards Calvary. By now their number was considerably increased for many pious men and women, whom the sufferings of Jesus had filled with pity, had joined them and they ascended to the west side of Calvary. There lay the terrible Cross, the hammers, the ropes, the nails and alongside of these frightful instruments of torture were the brutal executioners, half drunk and almost without clothing, swearing while making their preparations.

The sufferings of the Blessed Virgin were greatly increased by her not being able to see her son. She knew that he was still alive and felt the most intense desire to behold him once more while the thought of the torments he still had to endure made her heart almost literally burst with grief.

Chapter 12

The Crucifixion on Calvary

S even falls later, it was about a quarter to twelve when Jesus, laden with the Cross, was dragged into the place of execution, thrown on the ground and Simon driven off. The executioners now dragged Jesus up again and led him from a mount about seventy steps northward down to a cave cut in the rock. It looked as if it was intended for a cellar. They opened the door and pushed him down so unmercifully but for a miracle his knees would have been crushed on the rough stone floor. I heard his loud, sharp cries of pain. The executioners closed the door behind him and set guards before it.

And now they began their preparations. In the centre of the place of execution, the highest point of Calvary's rocky height, was a circular elevation about two feet high with a few steps leading to it. After taking the measure of the lower part of each of the three crosses, the executioners chiseled out holes in that little elevation to receive them. They next laid Christ's Cross on the spot where they intended to crucify him so that it could be conveniently raised and deposited in the hole made to receive it. They fitted the tenons of the two arms of the mortises made for them in the trunk, nailed on the foot-block, bored the holes for the nails and also for the title written by Pilate, hammered in the wedges under the mortise arms, and made hollow places here and there on the trunk. These were intended to receive the crown of thorns and Jesus' back so that his body might rather stand than hang thus preventing the hands from being torn by the weight.

What an awful spectacle it was for his mother! The place of execution, the hill of crucifixion, the terrible Cross outstretched before her, the hammers, the ropes, the dreadful nails! And all around, the brutal and drunken executioners, with curses completing their preparations. The crucifixion stakes of the thieves were already raised and to facilitate ascent, plugs were stuck in the holes bored to receive them. The absence of Jesus while he was in seclusion in the cave intensified his mother's martyrdom. She knew that he was still alive and longed to see him and yet she shuddered at the thought that when she should again behold him, it would be an unutterable suffering for her.

Four executioners now went to the prison cave seventy steps northward and dragged Jesus out. He implored the Father for strength and offered himself once more for the sins of his enemies. They dragged him with pushes, blows and insults over these last steps of his Passion. The executioners soon pulled off Jesus' cloak, the belt to which the ropes were fastened, and his own belt. When they found that on account of the crown of thorns, it was impossible to drag the woollen garment, which his mother had woven for him, over his head, they tore off the crown, thus reopening every wound, and crudely seizing the garment, tore it mercilessly over his bleeding and wounded head. He shook like a leaf as he stood before them for he was so anaemic and weakened from suffering from the loss of blood that he could not support himself for more than a few moments. He was covered with open wounds and his shoulders and back were torn to the bone by the dreadful scourging he had endured.

The people stared and jeered and the soldiers, cold and grave, stood proudly erect keeping order. The executioners then furiously snatched him from the hands of his guards and dragged him violently into the circle. The holy women then gave a man some money to take to the executioners together with a vessel of spiced wine and begged them to allow Jesus to drink it. The wretches took the wine but instead of giving it to Jesus, they drank it themselves. There were two other brown jugs standing nearby. In one was a mixture of vinegar and in the other a kind of vinegar yeast. Some of this last-mentioned they held to the lips of Jesus in a brown cup. He tasted it but would not drink.

They pulled Jesus up by the cords, took the sections of the Cross apart and put them together again in proper form. How sad and miserable, what a terrible and blood-stained figure was that of poor Jesus as he stood on the place of his martyrdom! The executioners threw him down again with words of mockery such as: "We must take the measure of your throne for you, O King!" But Jesus laid himself willingly upon the Cross. Then they stretched him out and marked the length for his hands and feet.

There were eighteen executioners in the circle: the six scourgers, the four that led Jesus, the two that held the ropes and six crucifiers. They were short, powerfully built men, filthy in appearance, cruel and beastly-looking and their features denoted foreign origin. Their hair was bushy and their beard scrubby. They served the Romans and Jews. Two of the executioners tore from Jesus the mantle they had hung around his shoulders. There stood the Son of Man, trembling in every limb, covered with blood and welts, with wounds, some clotting, some bleeding, covered with scars and bruises. He still retained a short woolen scapular over his breast and back and the tunic around his loins. The wool of the scapular had stuck onto his wounds, cemented by the blood from the deep wound made by the heavy Cross upon his right shoulder. This last wound caused Jesus the most unspeakable suffering. The scapular was now torn ruthlessly from his frightfully lacerated and swollen body.

When they tore off his girdle, Jesus bent over as if trying to hide his embarrassment. His blessed mother prayed earnestly and was at a point of tearing off her veil and reaching it to him for a covering. God heard her prayer. At that same instant a man, who had run from the city gate and up through the crowd, rushed up breathlessly into the circle among the executioners and handed Jesus a strip of linen, which he accepted and wound it around himself. There was something authoritative in the impetuosity of this man obtained by God by the prayer of the Blessed Virgin. In an imperious wave of the hand toward the executioners, he said: "Allow the poor man to cover himself with this!" And without further word, he hurried away as quickly as he came.

As Jesus appeared about to swoon in their hands, they sat him upon a stone that had been rolled nearby, thrust the crown of thorns again upon his head and offered him a drink from that other vessel of gall and vinegar but Jesus turned his head away in silence. And now, when the executioners seized him by the arms and raised him up in order to throw him on the Cross, a cry of indignation, loud murmurs and lamentation arose from all his friends.

Jesus was now stretched out by the executioners. He had laid himself upon the Cross but they pushed him lower down into the hollow places, crudely drew his right hand to the hole for the nail in the right arm of the Cross and tied his wrist fast. One knelt on his sacred breast and held the hand flat. Another placed a thick nail that had been filed to a sharp point upon the palm of his hand and struck it with furious blows from the iron hammer. A cry of anguish broke from the Lord's lips and his blood spurted out upon the arms of the executioners. The muscles and ligaments of the hand had been torn by the three-edged nail driven into the narrow hole. I counted the strokes of the hammer but my anguish made me forget their number. The Blessed Virgin kept wailing and wailing in a weakened voice.

The nails, at the sight of which Jesus shuddered, were so long that when the executioners grasped them in their fists, they projected about an inch at either end. When hammered in, the points could be seen projecting a little on the opposite side of the wood of the Cross. After nailing his right hand, the crucifiers found that his left, which was also fastened to the crosspiece, did not reach the hole made for the nail because they had bored it a good two inches away from the fingertips. They consequently unbound Jesus' arm from the Cross, wound cords around it and with their feet supported firmly against the Cross, pulled it forward crudely until the hand reached the hole. Then, kneeling on the arm and breast of the Lord, they fastened the arm again on the beam and hammered the second nail through the left hand. The blood spurted out and Jesus' cry of agony sounded above the noise of the strokes of the hammer.

Both arms had been torn and stretched out of their sockets. His shoulders became hollow and at the elbows one could see the disjointed bones. Jesus heaved heavily and his legs were drawn up. His arms were stretched in so straight a line that they no longer covered the obliquely rising crosspieces and one could see through the spaces made between his armpits. The Blessed Virgin endured all this horrific torture with Jesus. She became as pale as a corpse and low moans of agony sounded from her lips. Meanwhile, the Pharisees were mocking and jesting near to where she was standing, therefore John led her to the other holy women who had stood at a distance from the circle.

The whole body of Jesus had been in spasm by the violent stretching of his arms to the holes for the nails. His knees being consequently and inevitably drawn up, the executioners now fell furiously upon them and, winding ropes around them, fastened them down to the Cross but on account of the mistake made in the placing of the holes in the crosspiece, the sacred feet of Jesus did not reach to the block made for them. When the executioners saw this, they again uttered more curses and insults and with horrible scoffing they cried out: "He will not stretch himself out but we will help him!" They then tied ropes around the legs and with horrible violence and terrible torture to Jesus, pulled the feet down to the block and tied the leg fast with cords.

Jesus' body was thus most horribly stretched. His limbs had been so violently distended and his muscles and skin so pitifully stretched that the ribs of his chest could be counted one by one. The whole body was covered with wounds, swellings, scars, bruises and boils, blue, brown and yellow, and bloody patches from which the skin had been peeled. His chest gave way with a crackling sound and he moaned aloud: "O God! O God!" His abdomen was totally stretched out and it was as if the ribs broke away from the breast bone. His suffering was too horrible for words.

With similar violence the left foot was drawn and fastened tightly with cords over the right and because it did not rest on the block firmly enough over the right one, the instep was bored with a fine, flathead piercer, much finer than the one used for the hands, then seizing the most frightful looking nail of all, which was much longer than the others, they drove it with great force through the wounded instep of the left foot and that of the right foot resting below. With a loud metallic sound, it passed through Jesus' feet into the hole prepared for it in the footblock. I saw one nail passing through both feet.

The nailing of the feet was the most horrid of all on account of the distention of the whole body. I counted thirty six strokes of the hammer amidst moans which sounded to me so mournful, so anguishing. At the sound of the tearing and moaning that accompanied the nailing of the feet, in her most holy compassion the Blessed Virgin became like one with her son and the holy women, supporting her by the arms, led her again from the circle just as the jeering Pharisees were drawing nearer. Mingled with his moans were uninterrupted prayers, passages from the psalms and prophecies, which predictions he was now fulfilling. In fact, during the whole time of his bitter Passion and until the moment of death, he was engaged in these kind of prayers and the uninterrupted fulfillment of the prophecies.

At the beginning of the crucifixion, the Commander of the Roman guards ordered the title written by Pilate to be fastened on its wood at the head of the Cross. This irritated the Pharisees and the Romans also laughed loudly at the words: "King of the Jews." After consulting as to what measures they should take to procure a new title, some of the Pharisees rode back to the city and beseeched Pilate for another sign. The position of the sun at the time of Jesus' crucifixion showed it to be at about a quarter past twelve and at the moment the Cross was lifted, the trumpet of the Temple resounded. The Paschal lamb had been slaughtered.

By means of ropes several of the executioners now lifted the Cross upright, while others supported it with blocks around the end of the trunk. They raised the top of the Cross forward until it was perpendicular to the ground and its whole weight was suddenly dropped with a tremendous thud down into the hole. The Cross vibrated for a long while under the shock and Jesus cried out aloud. His outstretched body fell lower, the wounds were opened wider, his blood ran more profusely and the dislocated bones struck against one another. The executioners now shook the Cross again in their effort to steady it, and hammered five more wedges into the hole around it. When the upraised Cross fell with a loud crash into the hole prepared for it, an eerie moment of deep silence followed. It seemed as if a new emotion of horror, one never before experienced, fell upon every heart on beholding the Cross swaying in the air and eventually plunging into place with a heavy crash amidst the jeering shouts of the executioners, the Pharisees and the distant crowd which Jesus could now see.

But along with those shouts of derision, there also arose some other shouts at that dreadful moment — sounds of compassion from his followers. In a touching expression of pity, the holiest voices on earth, that of his most afflicted mother, the other holy women and the beloved disciples and all the pure of heart saluted "the Eternal Word made Flesh" elevated upon the Cross. Beloved hands were anxiously stretched forth as if to help him, nailed alive to the Cross, quivering on high from the hands of sinners.

While Jesus was thus standing upright upon the Cross and the cries of derision had for a few minutes been reduced to sudden silence, the flourish of trumpets sounded from the Temple. It announced that the slaughter of the Paschal lambs had begun. But on the Cross the words of John the Baptist were being fulfilled: "Behold the lamb of God who has taken upon himself the sins of the world!"

It lasted for hours, the pain and suffering, the jeering and mockery. All this time the mother of Jesus, Mary Cleophas, Mary Magdalene and John were standing around the Cross between it and those of the thieves, looking up helplessly at the Lord. The Blessed Virgin, overcome by maternal love, was in her heart fervently imploring Jesus to allow her to die with him. At that moment, Jesus cast an earnest and compassionate glance down upon his mother and turning his eyes towards her, he said: "Woman, behold, this is your son! He will be your son more truly than if you had given him birth." Then to John, he said: "Behold, this is your mother!" And John reverently and like a true son embraced the dying Jesus' mother, who had now become his mother also. After this solemn bequeathal of her dying son, the Blessed Virgin was so deeply affected by the finality and gravity of the moment that the holy women, supporting her by the arms, seated her for a few moments on the earthen rampart opposite the Cross and then took her a little away from the circle.

Towards the third hour, Jesus cried out in a loud voice: "Eli, Eli, lamma sabacthani!" which means: "My God! My God! Why have you forsaken me!" When the most afflicted mother heard the voice of her son, she could do longer restrain herself. She again pressed forward to the Cross, followed by John, Mary Cleophas, Magdalene and Salome. The body of Jesus could be seen on the

Cross, pale, weak, perfectly exhausted, becoming more and more white from the great loss of blood. He said, and I know not whether praying in a voice to me alone, or half-aloud: "I am pressed like the wine which was once trodden in the wine press. I must pour out all my blood until water comes and the shell becomes white but wine shall here be made no more." Then with his parched and bloody tongue he uttered the words: "I thirst!"

Hearing Jesus' complaint, his friends begged the soldiers and offered them money if they would reach to him a drink of water. They would not do it but instead they dipped a pear-shaped sponge into vinegar from a little bark keg which was standing nearby and poured upon it some drops of gall. The Roman Centurion, touched by Jesus, took the sponge from the soldiers, pressed it out and filled it with pure vinegar. Then he stuck into it a sprig of hyssop, which served as a mouthpiece for sucking, and fastened it to the point of his lance. He raised it in such a way that it should be inclined to Jesus' mouth so that he might be able to suck the vinegar from the sponge.

The hour of the Lord had now come. He was struggling with death and a cold sweat burst out in every limb. Jesus spoke: "It is consummated!" And raising his head he cried with a surprisingly loud voice: "Father, into your hands I commend my spirit!" Then he bowed his head and gave up the ghost. His lips, blue and parted, disclosed the dry and bloody tongue in his open mouth. His fingers which had been contracted round the heads of the nails now relaxed and fell a little forward. His back straightened itself against the Cross and the whole weight of his sacred body fell upon the feet. His knees were bent and fell to one side and his feet twisted around the nail that pierced them.

It was just after 3 o' clock when Jesus expired. His mother's eyes grew dim, the paleness of death overspread her countenance, her feet tottered and she sank to the earth. When she arose from the ground, she beheld the body of her son, whom she had conceived, flesh of her flesh, bone of her bones, the heart of her heart, now deprived of all its beauty and comeliness and even of its most holy soul, given up to the laws of that nature which he had himself created and by which man had by sin abused and disfigured. She beheld her beloved son crushed, maltreated, disfigured and put to death by the hands of those whom he had come in the flesh to restore and redeem. Who can possibly conceive the sorrow of the mother of Jesus?

As the executioners still appeared to have some doubts as to the death of the Lord, Cassius, the subaltern officer, afterwards known as Longinus, suddenly seized by a special ardour, halted between Jesus' Cross and that of the good thief on the right of his body, and with both hands he drove his lance upward with such violence into the hollow right side of the body of Jesus, through the entrails and into the heart that its point also opened a little wound in the left chest. When he withdrew the lance from the wide wound it had made in the right side, a copious stream of blood and water gushed forth and flowed over his upraised face. He sprang quickly from his horse, fell upon his knees, struck his breast and before all present proclaimed aloud his belief in Jesus, who was indeed already dead and so there was no need to break his legs. Prophecy was fulfilled. Not a bone was broken.

The Blessed Virgin, John and the holy women, whose eyes were riveted upon Jesus, accompanied the thrust of the lance with a cry of woe and rushed up to the Cross. For Mary, it was as if the thrust had pierced her own heart. She sank into the arms of her friends, while Cassius still knelt on his knees, loudly confessing the Lord and joyfully praising God.

Chapter 13

The Scriptures and the Crucifixion of the Lamb

A fter the exodus and in the days before Christ came on earth, the bullock and the he-goat were offered with the daily sacrifices of the evening in the Temple. The lamb is sacrificed, his blood thrown on the horns of the altar in the form of a cross and his flesh placed to burn on the everlasting fire burning on the great sacrificial altar. On great feasts, after the sacrifice of the lamb, countless animals were immolated, the blood of each splashed on the four horns of the great altar. In fact, the Temple was a great slaughterhouse of innocent victims to foreshadow the awful, horrific sufferings of the victim of Calvary.

"It is consummated!" he said towards the end of his ordeal and in a surprisingly loud voice in the face of his extreme weakness and parched tongue. It was an expression of great relief. It was all over at last. His mission was accomplished. It was the fulfillment of the prophecies, including that of Psalm 22 given 1000 years previously by David: "My God, my God, why have you forsaken me? How far from helping me, from the words I groan! Yet here am I, now more a worm than a man, the scorn of mankind, jest of the people. All who see me jeer at me. They toss their heads and sneer: 'He relied on Yahweh, let Yahweh save him! If Yahweh is his friend, let him rescue him!' Yet you drew me out of the womb. You entrusted me to my mother's breast; placed on your lap from my birth, from my mother's womb you have been my God. Do not stand aside. Trouble is near I have no one to help me! A herd of bulls surrounds me, strong bulls of Basham close in on me; their jaws are agape for me like lions staring and roaring. I am like water draining away, my bones are all disjointed, my heart is like wax, melting inside me. My palate is drier than a potsherd and my tongue is stuck to my jaw. A pack of dogs surround me, a gang of villains closes me in. They pierce my hands and feet and leave me lying in the dust of death. I can count every one of my bones, and there they glare at me, gloating. They divide my garment among them and cast lots from my clothes" (Psalm 22:1-18).

Isaiah also saw and prophesied it all: "He had no form or majesty that we should look at him; nothing is in his appearance that we should desire him. He was despised and rejected by others; a man of suffering and acquainted with infirmity; and as one from whom others hide their faces he was despised, and we held him of no account. Surely he has borne our infirmities and carried our diseases, yet we accounted him stricken, struck down by God and afflicted. But he was wounded for our transgressions, crushed for our iniquities; upon him was the punishment that made us whole, but by his bruises we are healed. All we like sheep have gone astray. We have all turned to our own way and the Lord has laid on him the iniquity of us all. He was oppressed and he was afflicted, yet he did not open his mouth; like a lamb that has been led to the slaughter, and like a sheep that before its shearers is silent, so he did not open his mouth. By a perversion of justice he was taken away. Who could have imagined his future? For he was cut off from the land of the living, stricken from the transgression of my people. They made his grave with the wicked and his tomb with the rich, although he had done no violence, and there was no deceit in his mouth. Yet it was the will of the Lord to crush him with pain. When you make his life an offering for sin, he shall see his offspring, and shall prolong his days. Through him the will of the Lord shall prosper; out of his anguish he shall see light. He shall find satisfaction through his knowledge. The righteous one, my servant, shall make many righteous and he shall bear their iniquities. Therefore I will allot him a portion with the great and he shall divide the spoil with the strong because he poured out himself to death, and was numbered with the transgressors. Yet he bore the sin of many and made intercession for the transgressors" (Isaiah 53:2-12).

Psalm 69:19-22 was another gift of prophecy: "You know the insults I receive and my shame and dishonour. My foes are all known to you. Insults have broken my heart so that I am in despair. I looked for pity, but there was none; and for comforters, but I found none.

They gave me poison for food, and for my thirst they gave me vinegar to drink."

But his suffering and death was the *raison d'être* for leaving eternity to enter into time to redeem us all. He was the scapegoat of the Old Testament and the true Paschal Lamb of God prefigured by the killing of the Paschal lambs on the night of the Exodus when the Hebrews were freed from Egyptian slavery. But in the new dispensation, the Lamb of God was slaughtered to save us from slavery to Satan. But when Satan revolted in heaven against God's commands, there was a woman involved in that revolt and promised redemption. God said to him threateningly: "Because you have done this, I will put enmity between you and the woman and between your seed and her seed. She will crush your head and you will strike at her heel" (Genesis 3:15). Her seed was the Redeemer, the Second Person of the Blessed Trinity. It was a man and a woman who sinned in the Garden of Eden and so, it was a man and a woman (a woman and her seed) who participated in the Redemption (although the woman was not co-equal to the man).

St. Paul refers to the Old Covenant and the ceremony which gave birth to the New Covenant: "The first covenant also had its laws to governing worship, and its sanctuary, a sanctuary on this earth… But now Christ has come as the high priest of all the blessings which were to come… and he has entered the sanctuary once and for all, taking with him not the blood of goats and bull calves but his own blood, having achieved an eternal redemption for us. If the blood of goats and bulls and the ashes of a heifer are sprinkled on those who have incurred refinement and they restore the holiness of their outward lives; how much more effectively the blood of Christ, who offered himself as the perfect sacrifice to God through the eternal Spirit, can purify our inner-self from the dead actions so that we do our service to the living God.

"He brings a new covenant, as the mediator, only so that the people who were called to an eternal inheritance may actually receive what was promised. His death took place to cancel the sins that infringed the earlier covenant. Now, wherever a will is in question, the death of the testator must be established. Indeed, it only becomes valid with that death since it is not meant to have any effect by the testator if still alive. That explains why even the earlier covenant needed something to be killed in order to take effect and why, after Moses had announced all the commandments of the Law to the people, he took the calves' blood, the goats' blood and the water, and with these he sprinkled the book and all the people, using scarlet wool and hyssop, saying as he did so: 'This is the blood of the covenant that God has laid down for you.' After that, he sprinkled the tent and all the vessels with blood in the same way. In fact, according to the Law, almost everything has to be purified with blood; and if there is no shedding of blood, there is no remission of sin.

"And he, Christ, does not have to offer himself again and again like the high priest going into the sanctuary year after year with the blood that is not his own or else he would have had to suffer over and over again since the world began. Instead of that, he has made his appearance once and for all, now at the end of the last age, to do away with sin by sacrificing himself. Since men die only once and after that comes the judgment, so, Christ, too, offers himself only once to take the sins of many on himself, and when he appears the second time, it will not be to deal with sin but to reward with salvation those who are waiting for him... Bulls' blood and goats' are useless for taking away sins, and this is what he said on coming into the world: 'You who wanted no sacrifice or oblation prepared a body for me. You took no pleasure in holocausts or sacrifices for sin; then I said, just as I was commanded in the scroll of the book, 'God, here I am! I am coming to obey your will' " (Hebrews 9-10).

Chapter 14

A Medical Analysis of the Crucifixion

Crucifixion was a method of capital punishment commonly used among the ancient peoples surrounding the Mediterranean basin from approximately the 6th century BC to the 4th Christian century when it was finally abolished in 337 AD by Constantine the Great, the first Christian emperor of Rome, as a token of respect for its Christian symbolism.

Mount Calvary was held to be a place of defilement and ignominy as being reserved for the chastisement of condemned criminals whose cadavers spread around it, giving it a more evil fame. The cross was accepted as the most cruel and shameful way to inflict death and consisted of two beams of wood, nailed one to the other in the form of an X, a T or a +, but the last is the most familiar form used in art. There were various methods of performing the execution and usually the condemned man, after being whipped, dragged the crossbeam or patibulum to the place of punishment where the upward shaft was already in place. There he was stripped of his clothing and bound fast with his outstretched arms tied or nailed firmly to the crossbeam. The crossbeam was then crudely raised and fixed high against the upper shaft with the victim hanging by his hands about 9 to 12 feet from the ground. The feet were then tightly bound or nailed to the upright shaft. It was the most utterly painful and degrading form of punishment which assured that the victim died with the utmost indignity. It was customary to give an intoxicating drink to the condemned before execution in order to numb the pain somewhat. Relatively ineffective, I am sure, since, for example, morphine from the opium poppy, *papaver somniferum*, was not discovered until centuries later.

Professor Judica-Cordiglia and Dr. Caselli di Fano have both expressed the opinion that the bruise on the right shoulder was so extensive as to prove that the whole cross was carried, not only the cross-beam. There are also numerous markings which have been variously estimated from between 90 to 120, and which are clearly visible on the photograph negative of the Shroud, peppering both the back and front of the body from the shoulders downwards, all bearing the tell-tale dumbbell-shaped markings of the Roman flagrum, a short handled instrument with two or three loose cords tipped with metal dumbbells or pieces of bone which were designed to shred pieces of flesh with each blow.

Now, for centuries Christian art has depicted the hanging on the Cross with nails penetrating the palms of the hands. If this was indeed so then this would also have caused the nails to rip through the lumbrical and interossei muscles of the hands. In fact, assuming that the shroud is authentic, it reveals that they did not pierce the palms of the hands, but that the nails were driven through the wrists which are comprised of a sturdy palisade of carpal bones made secure by ligaments. So said, it is important to stress that, anatomically speaking, the wrist is considered to be part of the hand.

Dr. Barbet of the St. Joseph's Hospital in Paris, which in the 1930s was one of the largest teaching hospitals there, researched the effects of wrist-nailing at that time. He wrote his classic book *A Doctor at Calvary* in 1949. He was aware of the complexity of the closely-knit carpal bones of the wrist and was concerned over the exact point where the nail had penetrated. He felt that there was a likelihood that the small wrist bones would have been broken in the process, which was contrary to prophecy, and so taking a freshly and recently amputated arm, he held the nail at the point of entry that the Shroud seemed to indicate, namely, the wrist at the junction of the hand and the forearm at the proximal crease or bending skin fold of the hand.

He gave the nail a firm blow, and to his surprise, it diverted slightly upward and with renewed blows passed cleanly through the wrist. It had found a space which was already known by anatomists but was thought to be too small for a nail to penetrate. This he thought was therefore the only space among the wrist bones to accommodate a nail without breaking a bone. What he also observed was an immediate flexion of the thumb occurring at the very moment of driving the nail through the wrist. With careful dissection it revealed that the reason for this was that the fibres of the great median nerve which extends from the armpit to the hand were damaged by the nail. This would cause a mechanical stimulation of its branches to the opponens pollicis muscle which innervates the thumb, causing the thumb (to move inwards) toward the palm. A nail in the centre of the palm could never achieve this phenomenon. He referred to the Shroud. No thumbs were visible in either hand as they were laid crossed on his torso.

When in a simple experiment which I performed during a postmortem on a patient, I placed a nail on the skin in the same position, that is, at the midpoint of the proximal crease of the wrist, the anatomical position of the nail was clearly shown at x-ray to correspond to Barbet's space, which was lateral to the capitate and lunate wrist bones. A sharp-pointed nail, taking the line of least resistance, would also move aside the bones and widen this space as it pierced its way through. In so doing, it would certainly also split some of the fibres of the median nerve which courses along this precise longitudinal axis. On the Shroud the right sole of the foot is well-defined but of the left only the heel is visible, also suggesting that there was retention in rigor mortis of the position of the feet at death — the left crossed over the right with one nail through both feet.

Now, they believed that he was already dead and so instead of breaking his legs, one of the soldiers pierced his side to make doubly sure that he was indeed dead. "Immediately there came out blood and water." That flow of blood and water proceeded from an elliptical area measuring approximately 1 3/4 inches long by 1/2 inch high, the shape conforming precisely to what one would expect of a wound by a spear. It is generally agreed that this chest wound was in the space between the right fifth and sixth ribs in the side. The angle of the spear would have had to be oblique and it is reasonable to conclude that it avoided the liver. Medical evidence therefore concludes that Christian artists have also been wrong, both historically and anatomically, in depicting the chest wound on the left side, the nails through the palms and the right foot over the left.

The physiologist Samuel Haughton of the University of Dublin proclaimed many years ago that the flow of blood and water that emerged was "either a natural phenomenon explicable by natural causes or it was a miracle." That the disciple John thought that it was unusual, appears plainly from the comment he made about it, and from the emphatic manner in which he solemnly declared his eyewitness accuracy. But, there has not been a unanimity of medical opinion with respect to the explanation of the "blood and water." For example, Dr. Barbet first propagated the view involving the pericardium (the sac which surrounds the heart). This usually contains a very small amount of watery fluid, but under certain circumstances the amount of fluid may increase significantly, causing what is called a pericardial effusion. He was steadfast in his opinion that the blade of the spear passed into the right side between the fifth and sixth rib, through the lower part of the lung and pericardium and into the right auricle of the heart and that when the spear was withdrawn, the clear serum came from the pericardium, and the blood from within the right auricle of the heart flowed out.

But for this to occur, these fluids would then have to pass through the huge chest cavity containing the lung in order to escape at the chest wound. Moreover, it is manifestly unreasonable and anatomically illogical to conceive that the bloody contents of the inside of the small cavity of the right side of the heart, the whole of which is only the size of a closed fist, would emerge to produce an exterior flow of blood followed by water. But above all, the blood in the heart itself would have already clotted, or semi-clotted, after death. The normal clotting time is 5-10 minutes.

Now, severe and traumatic chest injuries, as were inflicted on Christ, are capable of producing an accumulation of haemorrhagic fluid in the space between the lining of the rib cage and that of the lung (called a pleural effusion) separating the two linings appreciably. Such a collection of blood in the pleural cavity does not clot even after death due to a well-known defibrination process and it is therefore more plausible that the brutal wounds to the chest caused such severe contusions to the lining of the chest wall (the pleura) and to the lung that a bloody pleural effusion ensued and grew larger as the hours passed by. With time and with the upright position, the red blood cells would then settle in the lower part of the fluid with a larger amount of clear serum at the upper level. If then under these circumstances the spear entered at the side between the fifth and sixth rib space, an immediate bloody outflow of blood would be followed by the clear supernatant serum from the uppermost level, thus explaining the immediate flow of blood and then water. To date, I feel quite comfortable with this hypothesis.

Much of the agony of Christ's Passion stemmed from the severe debility from his sweating, lack of water and great loss of blood. There was therefore a thirst; a thirst for water, and his tongue and palate were totally dry, the tongue frequently sticking to the palate. Hanging upright on the Cross for three hours, not only caused severe pain from the joints dislocated from their sockets, but also evoked the most excruciating pains from the increasingly unbearable darts of electric-like shooting darts from the nailed median nerves and those nerves of the feet. In addition, the great muscles of respiration, the sternomastoids and the diaphragm, also went into unrelenting painful spasms. The muscles contract violently and cramps are experienced in both the limbs and the trunk. So severe were the muscular spasms of the stomach that the abdominal muscles also tightened forming a hollow cavity beneath the ribs.

There was also a thirst for air like that of the asthmatic, the anguish of which can only be appreciated by such sufferers. Indeed, much of the agony of crucifixions stems from the victim's incessant quest for air as he is fastened to the cross by nails and stretched almost immobile. This caused a distension and enlargement of the chest of Christ because of his persistent and difficult inspiratory attempts to breathe. His ribs therefore became more and more visibly prominent as the muscles between them contracted. And so, as the Scriptures say, the number of his ribs could be counted.

Now, the only means of delaying death is for the victim to raise himself so that he could inhale. Unfortunately, the nail driven into his feet is the only fulcrum which he can use to elevate himself, and this, in turn, caused the most agonizing pain in the feet each time he raised himself. These up and down and writhing movements of the body "like a worm" were continuous for three hours. In fact, it was because of the use and importance of the raising of the feet to facilitate breathing that the soldiers broke the legs of the two victims so that they could no longer breathe. Eventually the heart muscle weakens and becomes flabby (like wax). Heart failure ensues and the lungs and the space between the tissues and the lungs (the pleural space) become filled with serious fluid. "My God, my God", he cried during his crucifixion. It was not calling God's name in vain. It was a cry of anguish and for help!

Chapter 15

The Shroud of Turin

Crucifixion was an utterly painful and degrading punishment which subjected the victim to the utmost indignity. Indeed, it has been described as a form of execution which vividly manifests the demonic character of human cruelty. This was aggravated further by the fact that quite often the victims were never buried but served as food for wild beasts and birds of prey. In this way the humiliation was complete. In Roman times it was usually executed on dangerous criminals and members of the lowest classes, and so, in the death of Jesus Christ, God identified himself with the utter extreme of human wretchedness. He died like a common criminal in torment on a tree of shame.

Now, the Shroud of Turin bears an image corresponding impressively with the Gospel account of the Passion of Christ. It made its first appearance in 1355 at Lirey in northern France. In 1453 it was acquired by Louis I, the Duke of Savoy, and his descendants at first preserved it in Chambery, the capital of his domains, and later in 1502 it was kept in Sainte-Chapelle Church. One year after the Blessed Virgin appeared in Guadalupe, Mexico in 1531 and left her miraculous image (which science still cannot explain) on the tilma of Juan Diego, during the night of December 3-4, 1532, fire broke out in the choir-sacristy of Sainte-Chapelle, which almost destroyed the Shroud. One side of the silver box containing the folded cloth became so hot due to the high temperature that a drop of metal, melting from the lid, poured through small areas of the cloth.

In 1578, the Shroud of Turin was transferred and it was placed in a shrine in the presbytery of Turin Cathedral until the chapel of the Shroud was built in the Cathedral of St. John the Baptist. It was permanently installed in the chapel there in 1694. In 1983, King Umberto II, the last king of Italy, bequeathed the Shroud to the Pope before he died. In fact, it is often not realized that the Shroud has only been owned by the Roman Catholic Church for the last fifteen years through the person of Pope John Paul II.

This Shroud is unique. There is no other burial linen in existence that bears the photonegative image of a crucified man. In fact, no other burial cloth with similar markings has turned up anywhere and most shrouds decompose with their contents. It is of pure flax, as has been confirmed by analysis of the threads under the optic microscope and the scanning electron microscope. There is no trace of any organic or inorganic coloring pigments on the cloth, nor of any chemical compound extraneous to the flax fibers. The imprints on the Shroud are therefore the result of a natural process which has still to be explained. Inexplicably also, only the surface fibers are involved in the forming of the image, which is seen only on one side of the cloth. Indeed, even in this 21st century, despite all scientific advances, we still do not know how to produce a result of this kind. Another very unique property of the Shroud image is that it is indelible. This is shown by the fact that despite the vagaries and documented vicissitudes in the Shroud's history, the imprint is as vivid today as it was over the centuries, whereas artificial images are unstable and in time disappear. It has been the same for the image of the Blessed Virgin on the tilma of Juan Diego in Guadalupe.

The imprints on the Shroud of Turin are those of a human corpse in a pronounced state of *rigor mortis*. He is just under six feet tall and of good physique. Images of the front and back of the head nearly touch in the middle of the cloth, suggesting that the man was laid on his back on the bottom half of the linen and the other half was drawn over his face and front. The fact that there is absolutely no evidence of decomposition of the body suggests that he was in the Shroud for less than forty-eight hours, in keeping with the Gospel account.

The image bears the marks of lacerations from a severe scourging and a badly bruised and swollen face. The chest cavity is expanded as of someone agonizing for hours to inhale air into his lungs. As for the crown of thorns, it was not a wreath-like circlet as is commonly depicted. Instead it was in the form of a cap covering the entire skull, and its thorns dug into the scalp vessels which are well-known to bleed profusely. There are thirteen blood flows which can be traced to puncture wounds on the head. The knees of the man on the Shroud also revealed extensive damage such as would be incurred through heavy falls. There were also two oval areas of excoriations in the region of the left and right shoulders, caused by the carrying of the cross-beam of the Cross. There was also clear evidence that nails were driven into the wrists and not the palms of the hand. Apparently, when the nail had pierced a certain anatomical space in the wrist it damaged the median nerve, which caused the thumb to flex inward against the palms. And so, no thumbs are visible on the Shroud image!

A nail was also driven between the second and third metatarsal bones with the left foot on top of the right. In addition to puncture wounds in the wrists and feet, there was a gaping hole between the fifth and sixth ribs on the right side, and upon close examination, clear serous fluid is seen mixed with the blood which flowed from the incision. Amazingly, with all of this violent puncturing, not a bone was broken as Scripture had predicted.

The Shroud also testifies that all across the back, shoulders, buttocks and legs there were severe welts, puncture holes and shredding of the skin from the flagellations with the Roman *flagrum*. This was a short-handled whip with two or three loose cords, hooked and tipped with metal dumbbells or pieces of bone and which dug into the flesh at every stroke. It is documented that whenever a thorough whipping was carried out, the *flagrum* rained blood across the courtyard. The direction of the scourges on the Shroud also testifies that two soldiers stood, feet apart, on either side of Jesus, swishing their whips. How long this took no one really knows, but experts have counted up to 120 lashes on the Shroud's image.

Professor Pierluigi Baima-Bollone, an Italian forensic expert, after analyzing full threads that he had extracted from the Shroud's tiny blood stains, claims to have positively identified human blood of the group AB. Indeed, this was the most common blood group of the Jews in Israel at that time. The Shroud was also found to contain different kinds of pollen and large quantities of molds. We know that the Shroud appeared in Europe in the late Middle Ages and a remarkable number of pollen grains identified on the Shroud has been found to belong to species found in Palestine, the Arab lands of Asia Minor, and in Savoy and Piedmont, confirming that the Shroud had spent time in these places. One is therefore forced to admit that the Shroud originally came from Palestine and Asia Minor. A close connection was also discovered between the vegetable traces on the Shroud and some plants in biblical times. For example, the cap of thorns has been associated with the plant *Poterium spinosum*, a diagnosis which today is indirectly supported by the presence of its pollen on the Shroud as demonstrated by the Swiss criminologist Dr. Max Frei.

An extraordinary photographic characteristic of the Shroud is its "negativity," that is, the imprints behave like a photographic negative. In other words, they are dark, corresponding to the areas in relief of the man's body and light elsewhere. Now, when we photograph something, we get a photographic negative on the film, that is, an image that presents light and shade completely reversed and also a spatial transposition which changes right to left and vice versa. From the negative we then get photographs that reproduce the object as normally seen. In fact, during the first exposition of the Shroud in 1898, the lawyer Secondo Pia was granted permission to photograph the Shroud. When developing the negative, he saw the features of a man appear in positive although it was a negative film. It was obvious to him that for a reading of the Shroud it was better to deal with the photographic negative as, contrary to the norm, the image was much clearer.

A sample of the Shroud was taken in the sanctuary of the Turin Cathedral by a team of world scientists. It was removed from a single spot at the top left-hand corner of the Shroud. Three laboratories specializing in radiocarbon dating were each assigned one sample, weighing about 50 mg. The results were announced at a press conference on October 15, 1988. The Shroud had been carbon-dated to a period between 1260-1390 AD! Given this result, it was thought that the Shroud could not therefore be the sheet in which Christ's body had been wrapped when he was taken down from the Cross. This surprising and controversial dating of the sample of Shroud fabric would suggest, for example, that the Shroud was created by a medieval forger who, inspired by the Gospel to the letter, must have tortured and crucified someone in the Middle Ages for the very precise purpose of constructing a false winding sheet of Jesus. A hypothesis of this sort is totally unlikely, unscientific and unacceptable.

Scientists have since argued that textiles subjected to high temperatures for sufficiently long periods may fix carbon, resulting in a possible radiocarbon rejuvenation of the specimen. As Dr. Thomas J. Phillips of Harvard University's High Energy Physics Laboratory, commented: "If this Shroud of Turin is in fact the burial cloth of Christ, then it was part of a unique physical event: the resurrection of a dead man, which would have irradiated the Shroud and changed some of the nuclei to different isotopes. More recently, Dr. Leoncio Garza-Valdes, a professor of microbiology of the University of Texas, USA, also discovered an organic "bioplastic coating" on the Shroud that had accumulated from the symbiotic activity of millions of bacteria and fungi, building up into a casing. Dr. Garza-Valdes postulates that this coating so distorted the carbon-dating process that the Shroud is actually significantly older than was thought to be.

But there are several aspects to the Shroud which loudly testify that it is indeed the cloth of Christ. For example, on the head of the man of the Shroud are wounds caused by a thorn-cap. This is something truly exceptional and there are no documents reporting any such head cap either among the Romans or other peoples. Moreover, after death the man of the Shroud was wrapped in a sheet. This was also something very uncommon in antiquity as in most cases the corpses of crucified men were left on the Cross itself, to be eaten by wild animals, or at best buried in a pauper's grave.

The recent discovery of the imprint of a coin on the left eye, discovered by Professor Filas and later confirmed by other researchers, is a valid confirmation of a burial usage at the time of Christ. The type of coin itself has also been dated approximately to the first years of the Christian era. We may therefore conclude that the probability is extremely high that the man of the Shroud is indeed Jesus of Nazareth.

Chapter 16

Mary Receives the Body of Her Son

Nicodemus and Joseph carried ladders behind the Cross and mounted them, taking with them a very long strip of linen to which three broad straps were fastened. Then by striking upon strong pegs fixed against the heads of the nails at the back of the Cross, they forced out the nails from Jesus' hands, which were not very much shaken by the blows. They fell easily out of the wounds for they had been enlarged by the weight of the body which, supported now by means of the linen band, no longer rested upon them. Abenadar the Centurion meanwhile, and with great effort, had been driving out the enormous nail from the feet. Cassius reverently picked up the nails as they fell out and laid them down together by the Blessed Virgin.

The sacred body was gently taken down from the Cross. This taking down of Jesus from the Cross was inexpressibly touching. Everything was done with such precaution and so much tenderness as if fearing to cause the Lord any further pain. However, when the blows of the hammer by which the nails were driven out resounded, it reminded them of that most cruel nailing of Jesus to the Cross. They shuddered, as if expecting again to hear his piercing cries, and grieved over his death, proclaimed by the silence of his blessed lips.

When the body was taken down, it was wrapped in linen from the knees to the waist and then placed in the arms of the Blessed Virgin, who, overwhelmed with sorrow and love, stretched them forth to receive the precious burden. The Blessed Virgin seated herself upon a large cloth spread on the ground, with her right knee, which was slightly raised, and her back resting against some mantles rolled together so as to form a type of cushion. The adorable head of Jesus rested upon his mother's knees and his body was stretched out upon a sheet. The Blessed Virgin was overwhelmed with sorrow and love. Once more, and for the last time, did she hold in her arms the body of her most beloved son to whom she had been unable to give any testimony of love during the long hours of his martyrdom. She gazed upon his wounds and fondly embraced his blood-stained cheeks.

Love and grief in equal degrees struggled in the breast of the mother. She held in her arms the body of her beloved son whose long martyrdom she was now able to soothe by her loving ministrations but at the same time she beheld the frightful maltreatment exerted upon it. She gazed upon his wounds now so close before her eyes and she pressed her lips to his blood-stained sheet.

The Blessed Virgin's courage and fortitude in the midst of her inexpressible anguish were unshaken. She immediately began lovingly and carefully to wash and purify his body from every trace of ill treatment. With great care she opened the crown of thorns from the back and, with the assistance of others, removed it from Jesus' head. Some of the thorns had penetrated quite deeply. Then with a pair of round, yellow pincers, Mary drew out the long splinters and sharp thorns still sunken in the Lord's head and showed them sadly and slowly to the compassionate friends standing around. The thorns were laid beside the crown although some of them may have been kept as tokens of remembrance.

The divine face of Jesus was scarcely recognizable, so disfigured was he by the wounds with which it was covered. His beard and hair were matted together with blood. Mary then carefully and lovingly washed his head and face and passed damp sponges on his head to remove the congealed blood. As she proceeded in her pious work, the extent of the awful cruelty which had been inflicted upon her Jesus became more and more apparent and caused in her soul, emotions of motherly horror, compassion and tenderness which increased progressively as she passed from one wound to another.

She tenderly washed the wounds of his head, the eyes filled with blood, his nostrils and ears with a sponge and a small piece of linen spread over the fingers of her right hand. And then she gently cleaned, in a similar manner, his half-opened mouth, his tongue, the teeth, and lips. She then lovingly divided the remains of his hair into three parts, one part falling over each temple, and the third over the back of his head. As she disentangled the front of his hair and smoothed it, she tenderly passed it between his ears.

When his head was thoroughly cleansed, she covered it with a veil, after having kissed the sacred cheeks of her dear son. She then turned her attention to his neck, shoulders, chest, back, arms, and pierced hands. All the bones of his chest and joints were dislocated and could not be bent. There was that large and most frightful wound on the right shoulder which had borne the weight of the Cross, and all the upper parts of his body were covered with bruises and deep wounds from the vicious blows of the scourgers. On the left breast there was a small wound where the point of the lance had come out, while on the right side there was the large and gaping wound made by the lance, which had pierced the heart through and through. While doing so, her little hand covered with the linen veil entered almost completely into the large hole of the wound. Mary bent to see with dim light the hole which was formed. She saw the chest torn open and the heart of her son. She utters a loud cry. A sword seems to have pierced her own heart. She shouted and then threw herself on her son and she seems as if dead.

The sacred body still laid in Mary's lap, bluish white, and with the red places where the skin had been torn off. She covered all these parts as they were washed and embalmed the wounds. I saw her taking the hands of Jesus in her own hands, reverently kissing them and filling the wide wounds made by the nails with an ointment. The ears, nostrils and wounds of Jesus' side she likewise filled with the same. She repeatedly wiped and anointed them but only to bedew them again with her tears as she often knelt with her face pressed upon them.

When she had anointed all the wounds, she bound up his sacred head in linen and with gentle pressure, she closed the half-closed eyes of Jesus and kept her hand upon them for a long while. Then she closed his mouth, embraced the sacred body of her son and weeping bitter tears, allowed her face to rest upon his.

Maria Valtorta's visions of what occurred at this stage are now quoted. Mary, supported by her holy women, goes down towards the sepulcher. It is a room dug into a stone at the end of a garden all in blossom. It looks like a grotto but it is evident that it has been dug by man. In the middle of it there is a slab of stone for anointing. Jesus was placed on it, enveloped in his sheet. John and Mary enter. The two bearers uncover Jesus but Mary never tired of caressing those frozen limbs with even greater delicacy as if she were touching those of a newborn babe. She takes the poor tortured hands, caresses them in her own, kisses the fingers and stretches them. She tries to close the gaping wounds as if to doctor them so that they may not ache so much. She presses those hands against her cheeks and moans and moans and moans in her dreadful grief. Then she suddenly asserts herself and says to those present in a loud almost commanding voice: "Go away. I will stay. Close me in here with him. I will wait for him. You will come back in three days' time and we will go out together. The world will be beautiful in the light of his risen smile!"

Nicodemus and Joseph approached her, laying vases and bandages on the clean shroud and a basin of water and what looks like lint wads. Mary notices it and asks in a loud voice: "What are you doing? What do you want? To prepare him? For what? Leave him in the lap of his mother. If I succeed in warming him up, he will rise sooner. If I succeed in consoling the Father and in comforting him for the deicide hatred, the Father will forgive sooner and he will come back sooner."

Mary knelt down by the head of Jesus and placed beneath it a piece of very fine linen which she had worn around her neck under her cloak. Assisted by the holy women, she placed on his shoulders bundles of herbs, spices, and sweet-scented powder and then strongly bound this piece of linen around his head and shoulders. She washed all these wounds, and washed and bathed his sacred feet with tears and wiped them with her hair. His head, bosom and feet were now washed and the sacred body, which was covered all over with brown-stains and red marks in those many places where the skin had been completely torn off and which were of a cyanotic-white colour, was resting on the knees of Mary. She covered the parts of his torn and mangled body which she had washed with her veil and then proceeded to embalm all the wounds.

The holy women knelt by her side and in turn presented to her a box, out of which she took some precious ointment and with it filled and covered the wounds. She also anointed his hair, and then, taking the sacred hands of Jesus in her left hand, respectfully kissed them and filled the large wounds made by the nails with this ointment. She likewise filled his ears, nostrils and the wounds at his side with this same precious mixture.

When the mother had filled all the wounds with ointment, she wrapped his head in linen cloths but she did not as yet cover his face. She closed the half-opened eyes of Jesus and with his eyes closed, kept her hand upon them for some time. She then closed his mouth and embraced the sacred body of her beloved son, again pressing her face ever so fondly and reverently upon him--bone of her bones and flesh of her flesh.

Joseph and Nicodemus had been waiting for some time when John drew near to her and besought her to permit the body of her son to be taken from her so that the embalmment might be completed as the Sabbath was close at hand. Once more did Mary embrace the sacred body of Jesus and utter her farewells with most touching words of love. It was only after some time that she allowed the men to lift him from her arms and they carried him to some distance away from her. She then stands up distressed while they envelop him in a sheet. The deep sorrow of Mary had been for the time being assuaged by the feelings of love and his sorrow beseeching: "O, please do it gently!" The reverence with which she had accomplished her sacred task had calmed her but now once more deep sorrow overwhelmed her and she fell into the arms of the holy women.

The sorrowful mother is now almost raving. "It will be easier for him to rise if he is free from those funereal useless bandages. Why are you looking at me so, Joseph? And you, Nicodemus? Even an adulterous generation who asks for a sign will be given no other sign but that of Jonah. And so, the Son of Man will spend three days and three nights in the heart of the earth. Do you not remember? 'Destroy this temple of the true God and in three days I will rebuild it.' Are you pitying me? Do you think that I am insane? What? He raised the dead and will he not be able to raise himself?"

"Ah! he is biting at my heart!" cried Mary. "Who mother?"

asked John. "O John! It is Satan! Satan who is saying: 'He will not rise. No prophet said that.' O Most High God! Help me all of you. My reason is wavering! I do not remember anything anymore. What do the prophets say? What does the psalm say? O! who will repeat to me the passages which speak of my Jesus?" It is the Magdalene, who, in her melodious voice, recites David's psalm on the Passion of the Messiah (Psalm 22).

Supported by John, Mary weeps more bitterly and her tears fall on her dead son, wetting him completely. She notices it and wipes him saying in a loud voice: "So many tears. And when you were so thirsty I could not give you even one drop. You have tasted so much bitterness! Do not also let all the bitterness and the salt of your mother's tears fall on your wounded lips. Should I not believe your holy word? Who, tell my soul! Speak to my anxious soul. Tell your mother that you are coming back. Say: 'On the third day I will rise from the dead.'"

"Come, Mother!" This time it is the Magdalene who said so as she planned to take Mary from her son and to separate Jesus' fingers which are interlaced with Mary's. The mother straightens herself up. She is impressive. For the last time she stretches out the poor bloodless fingers and lays his inert hand along the side of the body. Then she lowers her arms towards the ground, and standing upright, her head bent slightly back, she prays and offers. Not a word is heard but from her whole appearance it is evident that she is praying. She is really the Priestess at the altar; the Priestess at the moment of the Offertory. Then she turns around and says: "You may continue. But he will rise from the dead." Mary was the only one who continued to believe.

They take away the poor mother, who goes off looking back to see her Jesus, who is left alone in the dark sepulchre. They rolled the sepulchral stone into its lodging. Some long branches of a ruffled rose-bush hanging from the top of the grotto towards the ground seem to be knocking at the stone door as if saying: "Why are you closing before a weeping mother?" They also seem to be weeping drops of blood as they shed their red petals and their corollas lay along the dark stone. The closed buds knock against the inexorable door.

Mary, who so far has been supported by John and has been sobbing rather quietly, frees herself from the apostle and with a cry, which I think makes the very fibers of the plants quiver, throws herself against the entrance. She gets hold of the protruding sepulchral stone to shift it. She skins her fingers and breaks her nails without being successful and even tries to prize the rough stone with her head. Being wild and frantic out of motherly love, her cry sounds like a lioness that wounds herself struggling near a trap in which her little ones are closed. There is nothing left in her of the meek virgin of Nazareth, of the patient woman known so far. She is the mother; simply a mother attached to her child with all the fibers and nerves of her body and of her love. She is the most true mistress of that body, to which she has given birth, the only mistress, after God, and she does not want to be robbed of her property. She is the Queen who is defending her crown, her son. She does not rebel. She only asks the stone to move aside to let her go in because her place is in there where he is!

Mary asks them to obey her and to open the sepulchre. After striking and staining the unrelenting stone with the blood of her lips and fingers, she turns around, leans against it with her arms outstretched, gripping the two edges of the stone once again, and solemn in her majesty, she orders: "Open it! Here is my bread and my bed. Here is my abode. I have no other home, no other purpose. You may go." They tried to detach her hands from the stone but they are frightened of those eyes, which they have never seen before, flashing in such a way that makes them look glassy and florescent. This is a new Mary.

But her will and imperious commands soon vanish. Her eyes become meek once more like those of a tortured dove. Her gestures are no longer imposing and she lowers her head in a beseeching attitude, and joining her hands, she begged them: "O, do leave me! For the sake of your dead relatives, for the sake of the living ones that you love, have mercy on a poor mother! My Jesus, my little Jesus, my child!"

It is the Magdalene who finds a reason capable of bending the sorrowful mother to obedience: "You are good and you are holy and you believe and you are strong. But what are we? Those who remain are trembling. The doubt, which is already in us, will overwhelm us. You are the mother. You not only have the duties and rights on your son, but also the duties and rights on what belongs to your son. You must come back with us, among us, to reassure us, to infuse your faith into us. Mother of my Saviour, come back with us since you are the love of God, to give us this love of yours. Do you want poor Mary of Magdalene to get lost again after he saved her with so much pity?"

Mary then replies softly: "No. I will be reproached for that. You are right. I must go back and look for the apostles, the disciples, the relatives, everybody, and say: 'Have faith.' Say: 'He forgives you.'" She stands up and leaves the half-dark garden. The guards guarding the tomb looked at them without saying anything. The town seems to be forlorn as nothing but silence comes from it.

Chapter 17

Satan's Reaction to His Defeat by Jesus and Mary

In Chapter XXIII of the *City of God*, the Venerable Maria de Jesus de Agreda wrote about other revelations which she had received and about which other mystics have not written. With respect to the triumph of Christ over Satan by his death, she wrote that it was revealed by the Blessed Virgin to her that Lucifer and his demons in the course of the life and miracles of Jesus never could ascertain fully whether he was truly God and Redeemer of the world and consequently what was also the true status and dignity of Mary. But this was so disposed by Divine Providence in order that the whole mystery of the Incarnation and the Redemption of the human race might be more fittingly and readily accomplished. And so, Lucifer, although knowing that the Second Person was going to assume human flesh, nevertheless knew nothing of the manner and the circumstances of the Incarnation.

As he formed an opinion of this mystery in accordance with his pride, he was full of presumptions, sometimes believing Christ to be God on account of his miracles and sometimes rejecting such an opinion on account of seeing him poor, humiliated, afflicted and fatigued. Harassed by these contradicting evidences, he remained in doubt and actually continued his doubt until the hour of Christ's death on the Cross when, in virtue of the Passion and death of that sacred humanity, which he had himself brought about, he was to be both deceived and vanquished.

In the sixth word of Jesus: "It is consummated!" Lucifer and his hordes were now aware that the mystery of the Incarnation and Redemption was now accomplished and entirely perfected according to the decree of the Divine Wisdom for they then realized that Christ had obediently fulfilled the will of the Eternal Father; that he had accomplished all the prophecies made to the world by the ancient prophets; that his humility and obedience had compensated for their own pride and disobedience in heaven in not having sub-jected himself and acknowledged Christ as his superior in human flesh; and that they were now, through the wisdom of God, to be humbled and vanquished by the very Lord, who they despised. They realized that by his death he put an end to the power of death, overcame it, and that it was the death of death itself. All this was fulfilled to the letter. Lucifer was crushed under the feet of Christ and his blessed mother, who subdued him by their sufferings and obedience. The prophecy and scold of Genesis 3:15 was fulfilled: "I will put enmity between you and the woman, between your seed and her seed. She will crush your head."

When Lucifer recovered from his consternation, in his pride he set about proposing to his fellow-demons new plans. For this purpose, he called them all together and placing himself in an el-evated position, he spoke to them: "To you, who have for so many ages followed and still follow my standards for the vengeance of my wrongs, is known the injury which I have now sustained at the hand of this man-God and how for 33 years he led me about in deceit, hiding his divinity and concealing the operations of his soul. Now he has triumphed by the very death which we have brought upon him. Before he assumed flesh I hated him and refused to acknowledge him as being more worthy than I to be adored by the rest of creation. Although on account of this resistance I was cast out from heaven with you and was degraded into this abominable condition so unworthy of my greatness and former beauty, I am even more tormented to see myself thus vanquished and oppressed by this man and by his mother.

"From the day in which the first mortals were created, I have sleeplessly sought to find them and destroy them or if I should not be able to destroy them, I, at least, wished to bring destruction upon all his creatures and induce them not to acknowledge him as their God and that none of them should ever draw any benefit from his works. This has been my intent and to this all my solicitude and efforts were directed. But all in vain since he has overcome me by his humility and poverty, crushed me by his patience, and at last has despoiled me of the sovereignty of the world by his Passion and death, thus causing me such excruciating pain in that even if I had succeeded in hurling him from the right hand of his Father where he sits triumphant, and if I should draw all the souls redeemed down into this hell, my wrath would not be satisfied or my fury placated.

Now, after a long discourse of his woes as revealed to her by the Blessed Virgin, Maria Valtorta wrote that all the demons agreed to sow among men the seed of discord, hatred and vengeance, proud and sensual thoughts, desires for riches or honours, and to suggest sophisticated reasons against all the virtues Christ had taught. Above all, they intended to weaken the remembrance of his Passion and his death, of the means of salvation and of the eternal pains of hell. By these means, the demons spoke about their plans to burden all the powers and the faculties of men with solicitude for worldly affairs and sensual pleasures, leaving them little time for spiritual thoughts and their own salvation.

According to the mystic, acting upon this course of action, they distributed the spheres of work among themselves in order that each squadron of demons might tempt men to different devices and heresies. Lucifer showed himself content with these infernal counsels as being opposed to the divine truth and to be destructive of this very foundation of man's rescue. He lavished praise and high offices upon those demons, who showed themselves willing to cooperate.

The Venerable Maria de Jesus then added her own thoughts and wrote warning us: "Our enemy is astute, cruel and watchful while we are sleepy, lukewarm and careless. What wonder that Lucifer has entrenched himself so firmly in the world and so many listen to him, accept and follow his deceits, when so few resist him and entirely forget the eternal death which he so furiously and maliciously seeks to grow upon us? Beseech those who read this not to forget this dreadful danger."

Chapter 18

The Co-Sufferer

Close to his death, he made his last will and testament and bequeathed his mother to be our mother also, our spiritual mother. "Woman, behold your son… Behold your mother," he said first to his mother and then to John (John 19:26-27). "Woman, behold your son," he said to her. He was obviously referring to her as the "woman" first spoken of in Genesis 3:15: "I will put enmity between you and the woman, and between your seed and her seed; she will crush your head." Indeed, it was on this hill called Calvary that this verse in Genesis was fulfilled. The word Calvary is from the Latin word *Calvaria*, meaning skull. The hill was also called Golgatha, the Hebrew word from the Greek *Kranion,* a skull. The Cross of the Redeemer was firmly crushed into the ground. And so, the "skull" was "crushed" by the man on the Cross, the Redeemer ("her seed"), and beneath that rugged Cross was the

Coredemptrix (not co-equal); one suffering woman, suffering *with* God who in turn was suffering *for* mankind and *from* them. Redemption begun at the Annunciation was completed on Calvary. It was 3:00 p.m. on a Friday.

But do we really understand and appreciate what it means to be "at the foot of the Cross" for three hours? Hers was the most spiritual, the most intense and incomparable suffering ever known; one solitary creature suffering with God, who in turn was suffering *for* all mankind and *from* them. She was a martyr whom God preserved from dying! That was the meaning of being the second Eve. That was the price of being Co-Redemptrix, for from the very beginning of Creation she was thus chosen. But it was as though God had predetermined that one had to be a "Mary" to have the privilege of standing beneath the Cross. John speaks of that congregation: "Standing by the cross were his mother (Mary), and his mother's sister, Mary the wife of Clopas, and Mary Magdalene" (John 19:25).

Redemption had to come from suffering, and so, he needed a body to suffer. His mother gave him that body. No human father was involved in that conception. "You who wanted no sacrifice or oblation, prepared a body for me" (Hebrews 10:5). On that joyous day when he was born she wrapped his tiny body in swaddling clothes and placed him in his crib (Luke 2:12). But on that Friday at the foot of the Cross, thirty three years later, she received a body, tattered and torn and swaddled with blood as he took upon himself the sins of the world. It was not a pretty sight but neither is sin in the eyes of God! It was the blood of the new and everlasting covenant which was shed for all so that sins may be forgiven.

Her suffering too was minimized. Words cannot fully describe and adequately measure Mary's anguish on that day. Perhaps it can be appreciated somewhat better if every mother were to contemplate her own son on the cross in place of the son of Mary. Yet, if there were a thousand such mothers standing at the feet of a thousand crosses bearing their thousand crucified sons, the sum total of their anguish could not in any way equate the pain and suffering of that Mother of Sorrows on that hill on that Friday that some men call "Good." She too was being crucified!

So said, in 1373, Lady Julian of Norwich, in her book *Revelations of Divine Love* which records her privileged visions from God, says of Mary: "I saw part of the love and suffering of Our Lady Saint Mary, for she and Christ were so joined in love that the greatness of their love caused the greatness of her grief… for the higher, the greater, and the sweeter the love is, so the greater the grief it is for those who love, to see their loved one suffer."

What is also not appreciated by many is that spiritual and mental suffering can also be as agonizing as physical pain, and at times even more so. For example, the emotional pain of a patient suffering from depression and the spiritual dryness of the "desert", the so-called "dark night of the soul," which a few prayful people experience, can parallel or exceed physical pain, albeit measured on different scales and parameters of human suffering. There are also many cases, for example, of elderly spouses of happy and long-standing marriages, dying within hours or days of each other from the sheer anguish of the death of their loved one and from the unbearable and emotional pain of the separation. So it would have been with the Mother of Love on that Friday had she not been preserved from death by God. Indeed, the Church recognizes her as a martyr, the Queen of the martyrs, but one who was not allowed to die!

Neither did Matthew, Mark, Luke or John record the great anguish of the mother during the Friday evening, Saturday and early Sunday morning following the Crucifixion. In her book *the Poem of the Man-God* Maria Valtorta, the great mystic, relates what she was shown when Jesus was taken down from the Cross: "When on the ground, they would like to lay him on a sheet that they had spread for him, but Mary wants him. She opened her mantle, letting it hang on one side, and she sits with her knees rather apart to form a cradle for her Jesus. He is now in his mother's lap. With a trembling hand she parts his ruffled hair. She tidies it and weeps. Speaking in a low voice, her tears drop on the cold body covered with blood. She begins to clean and dry his body on which endless tears are dropping. And while doing so her hand touches the huge gash in his chest and enters almost completely into the large hole of the wound. She utters a loud cry. A sword seems to pierce and split her heart. She shouts and throws herself on her son and she seems also dead".

Valtorta then describes the vision she saw of what happened on early Sunday morning. Joseph had already died and now that Jesus, her son, was murdered, she was the only one left of the Holy Family. For her it must have been the desolation of desolations. Valtorta described Mary's longing for the company of St. Joseph to console her during those long three days when all around her, even the disciples, did not believe that he would resurrect. "Let me lean on a Joseph!... O, happy Joseph, who has not seen this day," she moaned. Valtorta then recorded her visions of the first meeting of Jesus and his mother after the Resurrection:

"Mary is prostrated with her face on the floor. She looks like a poor wretch. Suddenly the closed window is opened with a violent banging of the heavy shutters and with the first ray of the sun, Jesus enters. Mary, who has been shaken by the noise and has raised her head to see which wind has opened the shutters, sees her radiant son, handsome, infinitely more handsome than he was before suffering, smiling, dressed in a white garment... He calls her, stretching out his hands: 'Mother!' And he bends over his mother and places his hands under her bent elbows and lifts her up. He presses her to his heart and kisses her... With a cry, she flings her arms around his neck and she embraces and kisses him, laughing in her weeping. She kisses his forehead, where there are no longer any wounds; his head no longer unkempt and bloody; his shining eyes, his healed cheeks, his mouth no longer swollen. She then takes his hands and kisses their backs and palms, their radiant wounds, and she suddenly bends down to his feet and uncovers them from under his bright garment and kisses them. She kisses and kisses him and Jesus caresses her."

Valtorta continued: "Jesus speaks now: 'It is all over, mother. You no longer have to weep over your son. The trial is over. Redemption has taken place. Mother, thanks for conceiving me. Thanks for looking after me, for helping me in life and in death... I heard your prayers come to me. They have been my strength in my grief. They came to me on the Cross...They have been seen and heard by the Father and by the Spirit who smiled at them as if they were the most beautiful flowers and the sweetest song born in Paradise…These past days you have been alone, but that sorrow of yours was required for the Redemption… I will come to fetch you to make Paradise more beautiful… Mother, your kisses are a blessing, and my peace to you as a companion. Goodbye.' And Jesus disappeared in the sunshine that streams down from the early morning clear sky."

Now, in an apparition to the saintly Berthe Petit, a visionary who was highly respected in ecclesiastic and lay societies in Belgium in the 1920s, Jesus is said to have exalted the merits of the sorrow of his mother, saying: "The title 'Immaculate' belongs to the whole being of my mother and not specifically to her heart. This title flows from my gratuitous gift to the Virgin who has given me birth. However, my mother has *acquired* for her heart the title 'Sorrowful' by sharing generously in all the sufferings of my heart and my body from the crib to the Cross. There is not one of these sorrows which did not pierce the heart of my mother. Living image of my crucified body, her virginal flesh bore the invisible marks of my wounds as her heart felt the sorrows of my own. Nothing could ever tarnish the incorruptibility of her Immaculate Heart. The title of *'Sorrowful'* belongs, therefore, to the heart of my mother, and, more than any other, this title is dear to her because it springs from the union of her heart with mine in the redemption of humanity. This title has been acquired by her through her full participation in my Calvary, and it should precede the gratuitous title *'Immaculate'* which my love bestowed upon her by a singular privilege."

It was a man and a woman, who sinned in the Garden of Eden and so, it had to be a man and a woman to atone and make amendment for that transgression. God made that quite clear in Genesis 3:15 when he said to Satan: "I will put enmity between you and the woman; between your seed and her seed. She will crush your head." And so, it was to be the woman **and** her seed, and anyone who leaves the woman out of that equation is only preaching half the Scriptures, half Genesis 3:15, half the truth and a half-truth is no truth at all!

This ends a much abbreviated tale of the greatest love story ever told. Today it is said that the mother of Jesus is appearing all over the world beseeching us to return to God and not to let him die in vain. She comes, not to promote herself, but to lead us to him, especially in these perilous times in which so many of us seem to have lost our way. But as Jesus himself said: "I am the way, the truth and the life. No man cometh to the Father except through me" (John 14:6). He also said: "I am the resurrection and the life. He that believeth in me though he were dead yet shall he live and everyone that liveth and believeth in me shall not die forever" (John 11:25-26).